For Allan

Happy birthday!

Milton Tonkhin

Without Walls

Without Walls

A memoir by Milton Toubkin

Milton Toubkin

Matador
9 Priory Business Park,
Wistow Road, Kibworth Beauchamp,
Leicestershire. LE8 0RX
Tel: 0116 279 2299
Email: books@troubador.co.uk
Web: www.troubador.co.uk/matador
Twitter: @matadorbooks

ISBN 978 1788035 279

British Library Cataloguing in Publication Data.
A catalogue record for this book is available from the British Library.

Printed by CPI Ltd, Croydon
Typeset in 12pt Bembo by Troubador Publishing Ltd, Leicester, UK

Matador is an imprint of Troubador Publishing Ltd

To my beloved family.

Preface

Although I have made some half-hearted attempts to trace my family's roots, in fact I know very little about them. Nor did I question my mother and father about our family history. This is something I now regret, but it's too late to talk to them.

I do not want my son and grandchildren to be in the same situation when they become interested in their past. Hence the initial motive for writing this memoir.

To ensure that I did not allow my natural tendency towards procrastination to give me an excuse not to write, I joined a life-writing group through the U3A (University of the Third Age). They expressed a belief that my story, and in particular my views on education, would interest a wider group of readers. I also received lots of encouragement from my wife Marj.

Professionally, my most significant achievement was the founding of Southbank International School in London in 1979. Started with virtually no capital, the school was to be democratically run, with the curriculum based on using London as the classroom and determined by the needs of each pupil. Although things changed over the years the school thrived and became one of the most exciting international schools in Europe, truly 'a school without walls'.

Like most lives, mine has had its highs and lows. An impoverished but generally happy early childhood in South Africa; the divorce of my parents; my mother's suicide attempt, which led to my being sent to boarding school; bullying by my stepfather; going to university at the age of sixteen; teaching in Rhodesia until the Unilateral Declaration of Independence; moving to Europe and becoming head of two international schools in Switzerland where I also met my wife, Marj; becoming a father of two wonderful children; together with Marj, running a nursery school in England; becoming principal of an American school in London; founding an international school in London; the death of my lovely daughter Nathalie at nineteen; my son André's marriage to another Nathalie and the birth of our three grandchildren; and finally, retirement – these were the seminal events of my life. How they all fit together may, I hope, be of some interest.

The early years

The old man stared back at me with a slightly quizzical look. His eyes had dulled though they twinkled when he laughed. His brow was quite smooth, his hair, what was left of it, still had some colour except for his incipient sideburns, which, like his eyebrows, were a mottled grey. When he smiled – which he did quite often – his drooping lower jaw seemed to tighten and the creases disappeared, appearing instead around his eyes. Some veins and blotches were visible on his skin.

Best not to look too closely, I thought, and turned away from the mirror. What can you expect when you're over eighty?

On the day Edward VIII celebrated his only birthday as King, I was born in Selborne Hospital, Port Elizabeth, South Africa. It was 23 June 1936. I don't know why I was named Milton, but my middle name, Edward, is self-explanatory. My parents were Cecilia, known as Tilly, and Aaron, known as Billy. Don't ask me how these nicknames came about.

Dad was an avid reader (mainly of mystery novels) despite having left school at thirteen. Mom had completed 'Junior Matric' and in our circles was regarded as well educated.

I am not sure exactly when we moved to Pretoria or why. It may be due to my father's joining the army just after the outbreak of the Second World War. My earliest memories are of living in my maternal grandparents' rambling house in Minnaar Street, just around the corner from the Pretoria City Hall. The house is no longer there; in its place is a charmless block of flats.

My grandmother, Rebecca Levy, whom all her many grandchildren called Boba, was, when I knew her, wheelchair-bound. I remember spending many happy hours on her lap wheeling my little toy cars over her ample body. She never complained.

My grandfather was more distant. He seemed a rather stern figure and was very much the paterfamilias, although he was always indulgent towards me. Just two things I remember about him: he used to pour his tea into a saucer before drinking it and he always had his soup at the end of his meal.

In his home country he had been a master cabinetmaker. (This gene obviously skipped a couple of generations, as I hate DIY. My son André, however, seems to have inherited the gene.) When his first wife died, my grandfather married his late wife's sister, who was also widowed. Both already had children of their own. After their marriage and their flight to South Africa, they had more children. My mother was the youngest of their combined total of thirteen children.

My grandfather and Boba had emigrated to South Africa as refugees, fleeing the pogroms against Jews in Russia and other parts of Eastern Europe at the end of the nineteenth century. (I believe the family came from Latvia or Lithuania.) Once in South Africa my grandparents settled in a tiny remote hamlet called Hammanskraal in the northern Transvaal (now Gauteng) and ran a general store for the farming community there. That is where Mom was born in 1915. I do not know why or when they moved to Pretoria.

When the Second World War broke out (I was three at the time), Dad enlisted. Because he was in the army (though he was never posted overseas), my father was only an occasional figure in my early life, whereas my mother and I were always very close. I suppose the signs of the failure of my parents' marriage were already there, though I was totally unaware of it. For example, when he came home on leave Dad would sleep in my bedroom with me. I thought this was wonderful, not realising its implications.

Dad also taught me to ride a bicycle. The driveway at the side of the Minnaar Street house sloped down towards the garage; I used to ride my bike down the slope, but I always failed to brake and turn left into the backyard. Instead I would crash into the garage door. Once, in my frustration, I started kicking my bike. Dad got quite cross with me and threatened to take my bike away. The threat proved quite salutary, as I quickly learned thereafter to steer the bike around the corner into the yard.

I had two pet guinea pigs, which I greatly treasured. However, I had heard someone say that if you held a guinea pig by its tail its eyes would fall out. So I thought I would try this out. My guinea pigs did not seem to have tails, so I just held them upside down. Unfortunately they both died when I did this – I guess they died of shock or heart failure. Their eyes never fell out.

When we were living with my grandparents in Minnaar Street, Mom contracted rheumatic fever. She was ill for many months but fortunately, unlike my cousin June some years later, recovered fully. An interesting fact was the advice she was given by her doctor. He advised her to take up smoking! This was well before the serious consequences of smoking were realised. Instead, smoking was regarded as a good way to relax.

At some point after Boba's death Mom and I shared a house in Adcock Street with my Aunt Faye, whose husband Douglas was also away in the army. Faye had married a gentile. This was frowned upon by many Jews at the time, but as far as I know all our family just took it in their stride. Faye had two children, Rhona (four years my senior) and Jeffrey, who was eleven months younger than I. They were the closest companions of my childhood. When Jeffrey turned six (and I was still six) he and I danced around, singing, "We'll both be seven together!" (That I lost contact with them for more than sixty years is a matter of great regret, though it made our reunion when I was in my late seventies all the sweeter.)

In our back garden was a huge mulberry tree. Not only was it a great tree for climbing, but it also provided wonderful fruit. Above all, its leaves provided food for the silkworms that Jeffrey and I kept in shoeboxes in our bedroom.

At the age of four I was sent to the Iona Convent. (Jeffrey, who was just three, also came at the same time, but he screamed so much that he was taken out of school. He subsequently hated school all his life.) I on the other hand loved school. Our first teacher was Sister Margaret Rose, a young nun who I thought was the most beautiful person in the world. Sadly, she died a year or two later. Each child in the class had a small slate tablet, and we learnt to write our letters on this. It was easy to erase the chalk if we made a mistake.

At the age of six, I transferred to the local state primary school, Robert Hicks School. There, for the first time, I met anti-Semitism, which I just couldn't understand. (I still don't understand it or any other kind of prejudice.) There was also quite a lot of bullying, though I was never subjected to it. One boy in particular, who had six toes on each foot, was mercilessly teased. Robert Hicks was a far cry from the cosiness of the Iona Convent, but the latter did not accept boys beyond the age of six.

Fortunately, in standard three, at about the age of eight or nine, my mother transferred me to Christian Brothers College, which at that time was quite a prestigious school. Classes were enormous, sometimes up to fifty pupils. We sat on long wooden benches. In front of us was a long wooden tabletop studded with inkwells, which we would fill with ink (ink powder mixed with water), into which we would dip our pens and with which we would stain our fingers and clothes.

Even though discipline was strict and rote learning was the norm, I loved the school. This may be because I always did well at school - things must have been really tough for those pupils who were struggling. The strap was liberally used. I've always thought that the reason I'm good at spelling is that each spelling mistake meant one strike on the palms of your hands. Some pupils were constantly being beaten. Despite this regime I really liked our teachers, particularly Brother McEvoy who was funny and inspiring and Brother Dillon who was always kind and sympathetic. Only once was I sent to the headmaster, Brother Duggan, who despatched me quickly with a couple of strokes across the buttocks. Today such treatment seems barbaric, but at the time it was accepted as normal. Rumours circulated that some of the brothers sewed coins into their straps in order to inflict more pain. It was also believed that if you rubbed an onion on your hand after a beating it would make your hand swell up. I don't know if there was any truth in either of these beliefs.

Mom kept all my school reports, which always showed a pupil's position in class. Looking through them, I notice that at the end of my first year at CBC my place in the class was 4th, at the end of my second year 5th, and at the end of my third year (Standard 5) I had moved up to first place. I left halfway through my fourth year.

I used to cycle to school every day, sometimes by the long, reasonably flat route (a distance of several miles), at other times by pushing my bike up the hill behind our house (a very steep climb; the Union Buildings were on the slopes on the other side) and then freewheeling much of the rest of the route to CBC.

My mother was working at the time for Beckett and Murray, a leading department store, where she was the bookkeeper/senior secretary. Like many department stores, Beckett and Murray had a system of payment that I always found fascinating. When you bought something at the counter, the shop assistant would place your money and a docket describing your purchase in a small container. This would then be sent whizzing along a wire connected from every counter to the central cashier. The cashier would then put your receipt and change in the container and whizz it back to the shop assistant. All stores used to be buzzing with these containers shooting around the store. Amazingly, the system seemed to work very efficiently and you seldom had to wait long for your change. Of course, all goods were then bought across a counter. Serving yourself and taking your goods to a checkout had not yet been invented – or if it had, it had certainly not reached Pretoria.

On my way home after school, I would usually stop off briefly at Beckett and Murray or go to my piano lesson or visit one of my aunts or cousins. They played a great part in my childhood up to the age of thirteen, which was when I moved to Rhodesia. Auntie Baby (real name Beatrice) was my favourite. She worked at Natal Fisheries just a little further down Church Street (Pretoria's high street) from Mom's work. I especially enjoyed the wonderful pickles and the best garlic sausage (we called it polony) I ever tasted.

My aunt Polly had a flat at the other end of Church Street and I would spend many hours there playing with her son, Ivan, who was a few years younger than I. She had a wind-up gramophone with needles that could play up to ten records. We loved listening to the Ink Spots and the Andrews Sisters. She also had a toilet that flushed and central heating, both of which were marvels to me. Polly's husband, Tosh, had committed suicide by shooting himself. Apparently his tailoring business was failing.

Auntie Polly's block of flats had a flat roof where we frequently played. The caretaker's small flat was built on top of this. One Christmas Eve, Jeffrey, Ivan and I were playing on the rooftop. Suddenly we saw a figure in red descending from the roof of the caretaker's flat. It was Father Christmas himself! We were absolutely terrified and ran screaming back to Auntie Polly's flat.

Uncle Fred had a furniture store nearby, and I would often pop in to see him. I split my upper lip on a cabinet while running around his store – you can still see the scar.

My life very much revolved around my many cousins, aunts and uncles. This meant I never felt like an only child. We also had a great deal of freedom, riding our bikes all over the city, with never a thought of any danger from either strangers or traffic. That kind of freedom is almost unthinkable today.

Auntie Sylvia and Uncle Albert lived quite a long way out in Valhalla, one of Pretoria's newest suburbs. I would ride out there to play with their son, Neville. (Neville Eber became a world-renowned bridge, poker and backgammon player.) Their house was very modern, but what I loved above all was their collection of encyclopaedias. I spent many a happy hour reading them. For my birthday they gave me one volume – I thought it was the greatest present I had ever received. The following year they gave me Nathaniel Hawthorne's *Tanglewood Tales*, which perhaps sparked my interest in Greek mythology.

Next door to us in Adcock Street lived the Bender family. They had a smallholding, with cows and chickens. Like all the families in the area they had only an outside toilet. The toilet had a wooden seat with a bucket underneath. At the back of the toilet was a flap, and each day the 'emmer kaka boys' ('emmer' means 'bucket' in Afrikaans, and 'kaka' is self-explanatory) would lift the flap and exchange the full bucket for a clean, empty one. They would carry the buckets on a long pole, going from house to house performing this awful but essential service. Jeffrey and I always played at the Bender's house with their daughter, Helen. One day when Helen was on the toilet, Jeffrey and I decided to lift the flap and take a peek at Helen's bottom. She was terribly upset and it took many weeks before we were welcome again at the Bender's house.

An activity that Jeffrey and I used to enjoy was leaving a half-crown coin on the street outside our house. This was glued to a piece of string. As a passer-by bent down to pick up the coin we would tug at the string. Our giggling then usually gave the game away. One evening we were in our usual spot, eagerly anticipating the arrival of our next 'victim'. As he bent down to pick up the coin we tugged as usual at the string. To our horror and chagrin the coin became detached from the string. The passer-by happily pocketed the half-crown. That was the last time we played that game!

In the house in Adcock Street, which Mom and I shared with Auntie Faye and her family, the lounge was separated from the dining room by sliding doors. These served as the curtains for the plays which Rhona, Jeffrey and I regularly inflicted on our mothers and any other adults present. Our favourite was one in which we sang, "I will give you the keys of the kingdom, I will give you the keys of my heart." We enjoyed dressing up, and Rhona in particular liked dressing me in her clothes.

Just across the railway line lived the Jacobi family. Shirley Jacobi was my age and had lovely long curly tresses. I was totally smitten by her. Invited to her birthday party, I had saved my pocket money to buy her what I thought was a beautiful necklace. When I arrived at her house I discovered that I had lost her present en route. I spent the rest of the afternoon in despair, wandering the streets looking for the present, which I never found. I was too humiliated to return to the party.

Although I now visit the dentist with (almost) equanimity, my first visit, at about the age of five, was traumatic. When seated in the dentist's chair, I screamed and screamed. Mom was with me, but even she could not pacify me. So Dr Wronsky gave me a hard slap across the face. I immediately stopped crying and he was able to proceed with his examination. I suppose today his action would be regarded as assault, but it was certainly effective.

Sunday lunch was a big occasion. There were always many relatives present and we always had a roast. A regular visitor was my paternal grandmother, Leah Weiner. Occasionally we had pork, and I regret to say that Mom and Auntie Faye always told her it was veal. I don't know if she believed them, but she always ate a hearty meal in any case. Boba Weiner, as we called her, was a Weiner by name and a bit of a whiner by nature. She lacked the warmth of my maternal grandmother. She always questioned me closely about my schoolwork. If I hadn't come first in class or if

I hadn't scored 100% in a test she would always make a sarcastic comment. This used to annoy me, though at the same time it made me more determined to 'show' her next time. Still, she always gave me half-a-crown before she went home.

Boba Weiner was a widow. Her first husband had been my father's father, but he was reputed to have disappeared while travelling to England from South Africa when Dad was just a toddler. He was presumed to have drowned at sea, but it took twenty years before his wife was allowed to marry again. By the time I was born, Boba Weiner's second husband had also died. Many years later, when she was in her eighties, she married for the third time and became Mrs Schneiderman. She and her husband spent the last few years of their life in a Jewish old-aged home in Johannesburg. By the time she died she had shrunk to a little over four feet. Both Boba Weiner and her first husband were, I understand, also refugees from the same area of Latvia/Lithuania as my maternal grandparents. They settled in Oudtshoorn, a town famous for the Cango Caves and for ostriches. It appears that my paternal grandfather was an ostrich-feather dealer. Boba Weiner became a prominent member of the Jewish community in Oudtshoorn and was always very active in Zionist causes.

Another regular lunch guest was Auntie Ruth, not my real aunt, but a close friend of my mother's. One day, as we sat down at the table, she pushed her false teeth forward so that they stuck out of her mouth. Another terrifying experience!

Sometimes on Sundays we took the train from Pretoria to Johannesburg in order to visit relatives there. My particular favourite aunt in Jo'burg was Auntie Seema. She and Uncle Morris had two daughters, my cousins, June and Maureen. June and I were close in age and good friends. One day, when she was about ten, June was struck down by rheumatic fever, which gravely weakened her heart. For more than two years she was bed-bound. From being a beautiful little girl she became almost a skeleton. However, she had a lovely nature and never complained. She remained positive throughout her illness. At last she was allowed to get up and return to school. Alas, just a few weeks later she collapsed and died. We were all heartbroken, particularly Auntie Seema, who had tended her so devotedly throughout her long illness. Many years later, after Maureen married, she named her first daughter June.

Auntie Seema, by the way, was an excellent cook. She used to make a wonderful stew with breast of lamb. I have tried many times to recreate this dish, but I have never managed to reproduce the taste and aroma of Auntie Seema's stew.

On one trip to Jo'burg, this time by car, we stopped off in Irene to visit Doornkloof, the home of General Jan Smuts, South Africa's pre-apartheid prime minister. It is a simple, modest home, and is today a museum. While in the garden I picked a red fruit and began to chew it. It was in fact a red chilli, which seemed to set my mouth on fire. My mother knocked on the door of the house to ask for help. Out came Mrs Smuts, universally known as Ouma. She kindly took me into the kitchen, sat me down and gave me a glass of milk, which cooled my mouth, and then gave me a biscuit. Meeting her placed me just two degrees of separation from Winston Churchill, since General Smuts was one of Churchill's closest advisers during the war!

After the war, Uncle Douglas, Auntie Faye's husband, came home, but my Dad never did. Instead he settled in East London in the Eastern Cape, where he used his demob pay (that is, the money given to soldiers on release from the army) to buy the Gonubie Mouth Hotel. I was not told that he was not coming back, but instead the fiction was maintained that his work kept him from coming home.

Sometimes I spent my holidays with him, usually with Jeffrey and Rhona. (I don't recall how we got from Pretoria to East London – presumably someone accompanied us on the train, probably Auntie Faye and Uncle Douglas.) At Gonubie Mouth I met Stella Fletcher. I thought it rather strange that she lived in the same flat as my father, but just accepted it as one of those things.

During one holiday, when I was about ten, I was playing on the beach when the tide was out. I was sitting on a small mound which was surrounded by water, pretending it was an island. Suddenly, the tide came in. I tried to get back to the shore, but there was a very strong backwash. I was not a bad swimmer, but with the tide coming in and the backwash tugging at me I just got pushed further and further from the shore. Nobody was aware of my plight. Fortunately, a man who was a strong swimmer was further out and saw me as he was returning to the beach. He would push me forward even though I kept on being washed back to him. At the same time he shouted, and at last a lifebelt attached to a rope was thrown out to me. I was dragged to the beach and lay there panting. I was carried back to the hotel where everyone made a great fuss of me. I never discovered who my rescuer was, but without his intervention, I would not be here today.

Gonubie is a lovely spot at the mouth of the Gonubie River about twelve miles from East London. At the time, the hotel was virtually the only building there, though today there is a much larger settlement. The hotel restaurant had an Indian chef and Indian waiters. I used to marvel at the skill of the waiters who could carry so many dishes lined up their arms. The chef used to produce salads with beautifully carved vegetables.

One thing I loved at Gonubie Mouth was Dad's car. It was a two-seater Nash, with a dickie seat at the back. A dickie seat was on the outside of the car and took the place of the boot. Riding in this was great fun. I have not seen a car with a dickie seat for many years. Perhaps they are no longer permissible.

One year Mom came with me to East London, but we did not stay at Dad's hotel. Instead we stayed at the Langham Hotel in town. It seems strange now, but I never questioned the arrangement. Next to our room was a flushing toilet with an overhead cistern and chain. Further down the corridor was another toilet with a low flush with a handle. I always wanted to use this more modern toilet. Mom agreed, though she warned me not to lock the door. I ignored this instruction and latched the door from inside. Alas, I could not open it. In a panic I yelled and yelled. A crowd gathered outside the toilet, everyone trying to explain to me how to open the door. All to no avail, as I screamed louder and louder. Some started to bang on the door. Then suddenly the door opened – I must have pushed the latch in the right direction. Needless to say I used the old-fashioned loo with the chain thereafter.

When Uncle Douglas came home after the war, he and Auntie Faye, together with Jeffrey and Rhona, moved into another house. Mom and I moved to a one-bedroomed flat in Eland House, Church Street, right in the centre of Pretoria. This proved to be an excellent location during the visit in 1947 of King George VI, Queen Elizabeth, Princess Elizabeth and Princess Margaret, as their motorcade passed right beneath our balcony. It was during this visit to South Africa that Princess Elizabeth celebrated her twenty-first birthday and made her famous broadcast from Cape Town: "I declare before you all that my whole life, whether it be long or short, shall be devoted to your service and the service of our great imperial family to which we all belong."

When we moved into the flat in Eland House a new man entered my life. He was Ronnie Kelly, an Irishman. One day I found that he had moved in with us. Mom and I slept in the bedroom, and Uncle Ronnie (as I was urged to call him) had a bed on the balcony. It did seem a little strange to me, but I just accepted his presence. Ronnie was an epileptic and had quite frequent fits that were rather frightening at first. The worst thing about Ronnie, though, was that he drank too much. He would often come home drunk. I found this really repulsive, particularly as Mom would then have to put him to bed.

While living in the flat I used to go to weight-lifting in the studio next to our flat and to boxing in the gym across the road. I quite liked boxing, but was never able to climb the ropes that formed part of our training. So I always rather dreaded that part of the session.

Every Saturday morning, Jeffrey, Ivan and I went to the Capitol cinema (in South Africa it was called a bioscope) to see a western. (We used to call them 'cowboy' films.) My favourite films featured Wild Bill Hickock, and the ones I least liked were those with the soppy singing cowboys, Gene Autry and Roy Rogers. The Capitol was a beautiful cinema with a ceiling of twinkling stars, which for many years I thought were real.

Unlike today, there was always a strong supporting programme of cartoons (I loved Tom and Jerry), serials that always ended with someone hanging on to a cliff by their fingernails, whacky features like the Pete Smith Specialities, and of course a newsreel in those pre-TV days. The newsreel was usually inaudible because of the howling and whistling of the hundreds of kids in the cinema. On one occasion though the cinema fell silent, as the newsreel showed the dreadful scenes discovered when the concentration camps were liberated. I will never forget the sight of the walking skeletons and the piles of corpses.

Just as important as the flick (our term for a movie) was what happened afterwards. As soon as the flick was over all the kids would gather in the yard outside the cinema and swap comics. Most of us had very little money; so swapping comics was the only way we could get to read a wide variety of comic books. My favourite character was Captain Marvel. To become the world's most powerful man he would shout "SHAZAM!" (This stands for Solomon, Hercules, Atlas, Zeus, Achilles, Mercury, and gave him Wisdom, Strength, Stamina, Power, Courage and Speed.) The comics always contained advertisements featuring Charles Atlas. They claimed he had changed from a 97-pound weakling into the world's strongest man through an exercise regime called Dynamic

Tension. I often dreamed of doing this but never had the money or the guts to send for the details.

My most exciting holiday was when Mom took Jeffrey and me to Lourenço Marques (now Maputo) in Mozambique. We travelled in an air-conditioned train (which meant that you weren't choked by soot and dust) and stayed at the Hotel Polana, the most luxurious hotel I had ever seen, with a magnificent kidney-shaped swimming pool. (Many years later I saw pictures of the Hotel Polana, and what a sad sight it was, neglected and unloved. But today, I understand, it has been restored to its old colonial splendour.) But the greatest thrill for Jeffrey and me was a visit to the studios of LM Radio, where we met David Davies, a famous radio announcer (he would be called a DJ today). At that time no pop music was played on South African radio stations, which were all controlled by the South African Broadcasting Corporation. Instead, young people tuned in to LM Radio from Mozambique, which provided non-stop popular music, including the weekly *Hits of the Week from Mozambique* to which we listened avidly and which shaped our musical tastes. I was surprised to find that LM Radio's studio was a small room in a nondescript building, but nothing could detract from the thrill of meeting the great David Davies in person.

One day, when I was eleven, when Ronnie was drunk and being particularly offensive, I asked Mom why Dad did not live with us instead. She said that was because he was married to someone else. It was only then that I learned that my parents were divorced and that Dad had married Miss Fletcher. I absolutely refused to believe it at first, and remained both angry and ashamed about it for many years. Until my late teens I used to say this prayer every night before going to bed: "Dear God, please make Mom and Dad remarry each other and live happily together forever."

In the late 1940s poliomyelitis was a scourge which affected many people in South Africa. There was an epidemic nearly every summer. One day I returned from school and called Mom because

I had pains in my legs. Because of the polio scare she feared that I might have caught this dread disease, which was also known as infantile paralysis. The doctor was summoned, but fortunately it seems I was just stiff from a particularly strenuous weightlifting session in the gym.

At about that time Mom told me that we were moving from our flat in Church Street to a small house (in the UK it would be called a bungalow) in Buffels Road in a new suburb in Pretoria called Rietondale. I was looking forward to this, as it was an opportunity to get rid of Ronnie. Much to my dismay he moved with us, occupying one of the three bedrooms in the house. It was only many years later that Mom explained that she and Ronnie had been lovers. I should have known, but was rather innocent at the time, and could not imagine that anyone, let alone my perfect mother, could have any affection for such a drunk.

The house in Rietondale had a small garden, and I spent many happy hours hitting a tennis ball against the kitchen wall. Usually, I was Gonzalez or Drobny or, above all, Eric Sturgess, the South African tennis champion who never quite won a grand slam singles title, but won several grand slam doubles titles (both men's and mixed). We also acquired a Rhodesian ridgeback, Billy, whom I greatly loved. Dad was called Billy, and I wonder now whether our dog was named after him. If so, why?

Although I was keen on tennis, my great passion was cricket. During my years in Pretoria I did not have the chance of playing either sport, but I followed cricket avidly, read Wisden from cover to cover, and was a mine of information on cricket statistics. In 1948, the England team toured South Africa, and I was lucky enough to see the test match at Ellis Park in Johannesburg when Cyril Washbrook and Len Hutton put on 359 runs for the first wicket (a world record at the time), and my hero, South Africa's Bruce Mitchell, made eighty-six elegant runs. Sitting in the sun all day wearing shorts, I was so burnt that I could scarcely move. I had no idea of the danger of sunburn at the time.

Although the England cricket tour was the highlight of my year, 1948 had more sinister outcomes. It was in that year that the National Party, under the leadership of Dr D F Malan, came to power in South Africa. This gave birth to the doctrine of *apartheid*, the loathsome policy that made all laws on the basis of skin colour. It also established a hierarchy of colours: whites were on top, followed by 'coloureds' (people of mixed descent) and 'Indians' (which seemed to mean anyone of Asian origin apart from the Japanese, who were regarded as honorary whites). At the bottom of the pile were blacks, the native people of South Africa. Even today, the injustice of this vile system sickens me.

Like most Jewish boys, I used to attend Hebrew lessons after school in preparation for my bar mitzvah at age thirteen. What a dreary teacher we had! His only method was learning by rote, without any attempt at understanding. I managed to get through my bar mitzvah without a mistake, but what the chants and prayers meant, I had no idea. Unlike some of the bar mitzvahs today, mine was a very small affair, with just a few friends and family gathered in a side room in the synagogue, eating chopped liver, gefilte fish and pickled herrings prepared by my mother and aunts. I had hoped Dad would be at the ceremony, but he had driven the thousand kilometres from East London to Pretoria and arrived only in time for the reception. Reflecting on this now, I think Dad deliberately arrived late in order to miss the synagogue ceremony.

Although I am not sure of the exact time, at some point during my thirteenth year an event occurred that changed the course of my life. I arrived home and got a message to make my way to Auntie Polly's flat. There, several of my aunts were gathered, all looking very serious. Mom, they told me, was in hospital. Only later did I find out that she had tried to take her own life by running a tube from the exhaust pipe of her car into the cab. She was found slumped over the steering wheel by a passer-by and rushed to hospital. It took many weeks for her to recover physically. Why she attempted suicide, I do not know, and I have never felt able to ask her. The pressures of being a single mother and Ronnie's increasing alcoholism must have been among the factors that drove her to this act.

Guinea Fowl

As a result of Mom's incapacity, it was announced that I was to live with my father, who had by this time moved to Southern Rhodesia. He had sold the Gonubie Mouth Hotel in East London and bought a small hotel in Umvuma, a one-horse town in the middle of the Rhodesian bush. Umvuma was approximately halfway between Salisbury (the capital, now Harare) and Bulawayo (the country's second city). Apart from the hotel, the town consisted of a small general store, an 'Indian' shop, a tiny church, a primary school, and a police station.

To move from the protective environment provided by Mom and our extended family to Dad's hotel in Southern Rhodesia was in itself a shock. Stella, Dad's wife, did her best to make me feel welcome even though I resented her presence. Gail, their first child, must have been about two years old when I arrived. Now I had a little sister and felt immediately drawn to her.

Umvuma had no secondary school, so I was obliged to go to boarding school. Dad tried to get me into Plumtree, which was Rhodesia's leading state boarding school, but there were no vacancies. So instead I was sent to a new co-educational state boarding school which had been established just a couple of years previously. It was called Guinea Fowl School and was run by Lieutenant Colonel Douglas Ferrer, a tall, imposing man, well suited to the task of setting up a school from scratch.

The shock of moving to Umvuma was as nothing compared to my placement in a boarding school. Guinea Fowl School was a state comprehensive boarding school attended by the children of farmers, traders and others who lived in sparsely populated areas of Rhodesia where there were no schools. It was – unusually for a boarding school at that time – co-educational, and of course it was for whites only. The idea of having a mixed-race school had scarcely even been considered.

Set in a bleak landscape of thorn trees and scrubland, Guinea Fowl had been hastily constructed during the Second World War as a Royal Air Force training camp. The buildings were mainly a collection of wood and iron shacks sitting on raised concrete columns. There were a few brick structures housing the hall and canteen, as well as a purpose-built hostel for girls, who had recently been admitted to Guinea Fowl.

When I arrived in July 1949, in the middle of a term, I was taken to one of these shacks, which turned out to be the junior dormitory of Wellington House. It was a long building with about twenty narrow iron beds, every second one separated from the next bed by a small bedside cabinet. There I was left by Dad and felt totally abandoned.

Because classes were in session, the dormitories were all empty, except that in our dormitory there was one pupil lying in a bed, as he was not feeling well. This was Willie van Breda, the first pupil I met at Guinea Fowl School. Fortunately, he was quite friendly and thus eased my introduction to boarding-school life. When the rest of the boys poured into the dorm after school, Willie did his best to shield me.

How does a shy thirteen-year-old feel when dumped in a dormitory full of lively, noisy boys who all know each other and what to do? I can tell you: lonely and frightened, yet making sure that nobody can see that.

Those early weeks in boarding school were very lonely and painful. Loneliness and pain were not things that boys at Guinea Fowl revealed to each other. Instead, I phoned Dad nearly every day, using the little cash he had given me. The school had only one public telephone. You put your money in the slot, then when someone answered you pushed button A. If there was no reply you pushed button B to return your money.

Each house had a matron. She was addressed as 'Ma'am' (as indeed were women teachers). When I first heard this term I thought she was being called 'Mom' by the other boys.

At the time I joined the school there were two boys' houses, Wellington and Lancaster, each with three long dormitories parallel to each other. Separating the two houses was the ablution block, a dreary concrete building containing rows of toilets, showers and baths. Just across the narrow road from the ablution block was Stirling House, the first purpose-built house at Guinea Fowl, and this housed the girls.

To take a shower or bath we would strip off our clothes in the dormitory, wrap a towel around our waist, and walk across the concrete path from the dorm to the ablution block in full view of the girls. One day I had just had a very hot bath and was returning to the dormitory when I fainted and fell. At that moment the girls were lining up for their march to the dining hall. My towel of course came off when I fainted, and when I recovered I staggered back to the dorm naked. This caused the girls great amusement and me much embarrassment for some weeks after that.

The school provided all pupils with an official clothing list: so many shirts, so many pairs of socks, a tie, a blazer and so on. Our daily wear consisted of a khaki shirt and khaki shorts. Among the items on the list were underpants. But the reality was that no boy at Guinea Fowl School would wear underpants. It was regarded as 'sissy'. Teenage boys are notoriously randy and very easily aroused, especially in a co-educational setting. Thus there were frequent embarrassing moments, which underpants would easily have covered.

Because of the good grounding I had received at CBC in Pretoria, I did not have any difficulty with schoolwork, except science, which I did not like (especially after we had to dissect a frog) and woodwork (my lifelong lack of DIY skills attests to this). My other bête noir was physical education (then called physical training). Being rather plump and uncoordinated, I was constantly humiliated by not being able to jump over the gym horse or do handstands and somersaults. Nor, as I have already mentioned, could I climb ropes. One PT school report described me as 'pleasantly incompetent'. Fortunately, I managed to persuade Mrs Williams, the music teacher, to schedule most of my piano lessons during PT, thus finding an excuse to miss many of those dreaded classes.

My favourite subjects by far were Latin and mathematics. Mr Ian McLean, the Latin master, was not an inspiring teacher. He would sit at his desk, explain a new point of grammar, and tell us to get on with it. But I loved the logic of the language and was constantly fascinated by tracing English words derived from Latin. Discovering the word expiate (which means to wipe out, in the sense of wiping out your sins), I used it to translate a passage as 'Caesar expiated the enemy'! Later, when we came to study Vergil, I was excited by the tale of Aeneas, the vividness of the imagery and by the symmetry of the dactylic hexameter which Vergil employed. I still am.

Mathematics was taught by Bob Klette, a brilliant teacher who later deservedly became the Chief Inspector of Schools in the Federation of Rhodesia and Nyasaland. He encouraged me to take Additional Mathematics as a subject for the Cambridge School Certificate (equivalent to today's GCSE). I have recently learned that Bob Klette was famed in the South African Air Force for crash-landing a stricken Liberator aircraft in pitch darkness at Warsaw's main aerodrome during World War II.

For English, we had the Reverend Ivor Clark, who also acted as the school's chaplain. He was reputed to be a defrocked priest, but this may have been just malicious gossip. Although he was a rather lazy teacher, he had a wonderful voice and could read beautifully. Listening to his mellifluous Welsh voice as he read *Silas Marner* or played all the parts in *She Stoops to Conquer* and *The Rivals* was a great joy and turned me on to English literature.

Ivor Clark also taught us RK (Religious Knowledge). Because I was Jewish (indeed the only Jewish pupil in the school), I was not required to take this subject, but I nevertheless attended his classes and hit on the wheeze of writing all my notes in Latin. I am sure the notes were full of mistakes, but they greatly increased my ability to read and write Latin.

We were taught history by Tally Evans, housemaster of Wellington House. He was known as Snave (Evans in reverse). When he laughed he would finish his laugh with a loud snort. His teaching technique was simply to dictate notes to us, including, in the Cambridge School Certificate year, entire model essays on probable exam topics. 'Boring' is not an adequate word to describe his classes. But in my final year he lent me a copy of *Imperial Commonwealth* by Lord Elton. This opened my eyes to history and I could not put the book down.

Guinea Fowl was not a very academic school. Although those of us who enjoyed learning were not discouraged, the general learning environment was as barren as the wood and iron huts in which most of the school was housed. Rugby and cricket were what really mattered. I did everything I could to get out of rugby, and I generally managed to do so, much to the relief, I think, of the poor teacher who coached my age group. Cricket I loved, even though I was pretty useless at it. I once had the distinction, while practising in the nets, of bowling a ball that landed in the wrong net! My enthusiasm for cricket was recognised, not by selection for any team, but by my appointment as the official scorer for the First XI. The team travelled throughout Southern Rhodesia and I was taken along with them as scorer. When I finally left Guinea Fowl, my good friend Gordon Phillips (who incidentally was a much better cricketer than I – he bowled a mean leg-break) took over the role.

I used to enjoy tennis and squash, but these were not played competitively at Guinea Fowl and were generally regarded as 'sissy' games.

Although learning was not greatly prized at Guinea Fowl there were some very bright pupils. There was therefore some competition to come top of the class. The outstanding pupil in my class was a boy by the name of Lars-Olaf Nordejo. He was a brilliant Swede who was planning to study medicine at Uppsala University. Ted Hanssen and I were his nearest rivals, but although we might beat him in one or two subjects, he consistently came top of the class overall. I don't know what has happened to him, but I'm sure he became a distinguished doctor. Ted, I believe, is now in Australia with a large family of children and grandchildren.

Food was mostly diabolical, including over-boiled vegetables, powdered eggs, sago puddings with a horrible skin, and disgusting semolina. Some staff were strict about making us eat everything. Since I sat next to a window in the dining hall, the boys at my table relied on me to drop handfuls of cabbage and other unpopular items out of the window.

As pocket money we used to receive 1/9d a week. (That's about 10p without taking inflation into account.) This we could spend at the school tuck shop (I usually bought custard creams) or we could buy Cornish pasties and cream buns from a baker's van which stopped at the school every few days. Of course we mainly relied on tuck boxes from home. One of our favourite concoctions was tinned sardines with condensed milk.

One Christmas, I received as a gift a kind of racetrack. When you wound a handle, toy horses moved along and you never knew which horse would reach the winning post first. At the same time, a friend and classmate, Frank Delfos, was given a roulette wheel. Frank and I hit on the idea of supplementing our pocket money by inviting our fellow pupils to gamble on these two games. It turned out to be a highly lucrative activity while it lasted.

Unfortunately, Bob Klette, our maths teacher, and one of the house duty masters, caught us and banned everyone from playing these games for money. We took his words literally and thereafter sold tickets, which could be used as betting chips. Needless to say, although this ruse lasted for several months, we were later caught again. I don't recall being punished, except that our racetrack and roulette wheel were confiscated.

Sex education did not exist at Guinea Fowl, and we were left to make our own discoveries. For years I believed that babies were carried in a woman's stomach, which had to be cut open to release the baby. Many of the pupils at Guinea Fowl were the children of farmers. Presumably they knew how cows gave birth. While I could believe that a calf could emerge from a cow's uterus, it seemed impossible to me that a baby could emerge from a woman's narrow opening.

Although I was not aware of any overt homosexuality among the boys (in any case the word and even the concept were unknown to me), open masturbation (sometimes mutual) was commonplace – we called it 'tonking'. There were competitions to see who had the longest penis – Billy Trott (not his real name) won hands down. Another competition was to see who could balance the most on his erect penis. Willie van Breda could balance a cricket bat; most others could manage only a towel. Needless to say, I was too shy to take part in these contests!

One of the young male teachers was known to join in mutual masturbation sessions with some of the boys. Of course this is totally unacceptable, but as far as I am aware, the boys concerned willingly took part, did not consider it remarkable, and enjoyed his company.

Drugs, of course, were unheard of at that time. In the fields behind the school there were several antbear holes. You could climb down into these, and they were quite spacious, large enough to stand up in and to accommodate half a dozen boys. These hideouts were where smoking took place, though only a minority of boys smoked and there was never any peer pressure to join them.

After a couple of years, two new houses, Blenheim and Lincoln, were opened at Guinea Fowl. They were about half a mile away across the main Selukwe-Gwelo road and were based in the former RAF married quarters. Each house consisted of four small detached wood and iron cottages, each housing about twenty boys. Each cottage had one large room in which about sixteen boys slept, and then there were two smaller rooms with two boys in each (including a prefect). There were also two bathrooms. These cottages were much cosier and more comfortable than the large dormitories at Wellington and Lancaster. I was one of a group of boys who were transferred to these two new houses and ended up in Blenheim House, with the Reverend Ivor Clark as housemaster.

The day started early at Guinea Fowl School. We were up at six o'clock. Classes started at 7.30. This was a good idea, as school was over by one o'clock, before the often-intense afternoon heat. After lunch we were expected to rest on our beds until 2.30 when we would all trudge across to the dining hall for an hour's prep (homework). After that there were sports and other activities until about 5.30, when we took showers or baths before supper. Supper was followed by another prep session.

One of my closest friends at Guinea Fowl was Alan Ruffell, who was in Lincoln House, just next door to Blenheim. On nights when our Afrikaans teacher, Waggie Wagner, was on duty, because we knew he never checked the dormitories after lights out, Alan and I would often sneak out and walk the half mile to the main school, where we would visit some of our other friends, particularly Barry van Blomestein (an outstanding cricketer who was my hero at the time) and Gordon Phillips. Both were prefects in Lancaster House and so had small rooms of their own at the end of the dormitories. There we would have late-night feasts before making our way back to our own dorms. This went on for many months until one Sunday night when Bob Klette, our maths teacher, caught us in the lights of his car as we were walking back to our dorms. He had replaced Waggie Wagner that evening as duty master, discovered we were missing, and had been driving around desperately looking for us. I don't remember the punishment, but it was enough to deter us from sneaking out again.

All boys at Guinea Fowl had to belong to the cadet corps, which meant getting some sort of military training. We were taught how to march, salute, order and present arms and so on. This was one of my pet hates and I tried to get out of it in various ways. For a while, I was the bass drummer in the school band. I was not very good at it, I must admit, because nobody taught us anything. We were just expected to know when to beat the big bass drum.

Once a year we used to go to cadet camp at Inkomo Barracks, north of Salisbury (Harare), to which all the cadet corps in the country came. It was quite demanding but also fun. We slept in tents, sleeping on the ground on felt palliasses, about six boys to a tent. In the evening, entertainment usually consisted of boxing or the occasional show, but the days were spent marching around the parade ground.

The other way I managed to get out of the main cadet corps was by being transferred in my second year to the Quartermaster's Stores. This meant that I was one of two or three pupils who did not have to do all the training exercises. Instead, we were in charge of all the stores. Amazingly, the stores included many rifles, which we would issue and check back in, and all the uniforms, putties, boots and so on which were required by the cadets. Eventually, I became the Quartermaster Sergeant, a rank just below a commissioned officer. I quite liked this because when I went to cadet camp, I could sleep in a tent on my own or with one other pupil. What is more, since we issued the stores, we did not have to sleep on a single palliasse, but could pile them high, which gave us a much more comfortable sleep.

Guinea Fowl was a very isolated place. As I mentioned, it was halfway between Gwelo (now Gweru) and Selukwe, about ten miles from each. We did not get many opportunities of going into town. Just occasionally, we would be allowed into Gwelo. The great thing about it was that we would go to the Meikles Café, where we would order a Knickerbocker Glory, a concoction of ice cream and tinned fruit piled high in a glass. This was the highlight of our visit.

On Sundays, all students - at least all the boys - were required to leave the campus. We were issued in the morning with a small picnic, consisting of a slice of bread, some raw meat and a piece of fruit. We were expected to manage on our own. Normally we would go into the bush - the 'bundu' as we called it - where we could have a really great time. It was a kind of adventure camp, which we just enjoyed. We were not allowed back into the dormitories to get anything. Instead we just had to survive. It was actually very good for all of us. Usually we would slice the meat very thin with our pocketknives, then hang the strips of meat from the branch of a thorn tree or bush. The meat would dry there so that by lunchtime, or by the time we wanted to eat, we would have a kind of moist biltong. Some boys would make a small fire and cook the meat, but we had to be very careful. In the dry Rhodesian bush it would not be difficult for a small fire to become a large one.

Rivers and ponds in Rhodesia were quite dangerous, not because we might drown, but because of the bilharzia parasite, which causes a most dreadful disease. We were always told never to swim in rivers and ponds, but I have to confess that on a few occasions we did, particularly in one place we liked where there was a very deep pool. We would go skinny dipping there in the cool, refreshing water.

On one occasion we came across a small pond on which there were several ducks. The four of us decided that we were going to catch one of the ducks. Of course, as soon as we approached the ducks, they would fly a few yards further. So we decided that one of us would climb a tree and drop a large rock on the head of a duck. This we managed to do and grabbed the stunned duck. Our intention was to share the duck, not in order to eat it, but as a pet. When we got back to the school we drew lots, and I was the first to be allowed to take the duck home on our next exeat weekend. When Dad came to pick me up he was rather astonished to see the duck, but we wrapped it up in his raincoat and put it on the back seat of the car. By the time we got home to Umvuma, the raincoat was a complete write-off, the poor duck having messed all over it.

We looked after this duck for a few days and then took it back to the school. We continued to look after it, keeping it in an enclosure. At the next break, one of the other pupils took it home, but I'm afraid the duck never came back. They said it had escaped, but I rather fear it had been eaten.

Of course we were not supposed to keep pets, but nobody seemed to object to the duck. A pet that many of us obtained – and I was among them – was a little night-ape or bushbaby. You could find these night-apes in the bush, and they were really cute. We called them pookies. I used to keep my pookie in my shirt, because they do not like to come out in the day, only at night. Keeping them in your shirt, up against your stomach, was a nice cosy place for the pookie. They were generally very tame. We would feed them, of course, and let them out at night, but they would always come back because they knew, you might say, on which side their bread was buttered. I had my pookie for more than a year and really loved this little thing. One night, however, he did not come back.

It wasn't only my pookie that went missing. One day one of the boys in our dorm did a runner. He ran away from school, or at least he disappeared. For days the school was in a great state of confusion while everyone was looking for him. Police had been informed as well as his parents. One evening he reappeared. He had been living underneath the dormitories. The buildings at Guinea Fowl were constructed of wood and iron, and stood on stilts. So there was probably about two feet of space under the buildings. Thereafter we all colluded with him, bringing him food from the dining room. This must have continued for a couple of weeks until eventually he gave himself up. We never really discovered why he had run away, but he was not a good student, and I think he was just overwhelmed by the pressures of school life.

Although I hated rugby and was not any good at cricket, I was involved in a lot of school activities. I more or less ran the debating society and shared in the organisation of the school dances held every second Saturday. On the alternate Saturday, we had a film instead. This was shown in the school assembly hall with a single 16mm projector, which would often break down in the middle of the film, providing an opportunity for everyone to grumble and jeer.

I also took part in various dramatic productions. The first of these was *Les Cloches de Corneville*, a musical by Robert Planquette. It sounds French but was sung in English. Gordon Phillips, my great friend, had a leading part as Gaspard, while Hilla Schroder, with whom all the boys were in love, played the heroine, Serpolette. I myself had a minor role, but it had one great virtue: I had to play kiss-in-the-ring with a group of girls. Of course I was blindfolded and could not see them, but I would always try to catch one of the beauties and sometimes succeeded.

My second theatrical experience was in *Toad of Toad Hall*, A A Milne's adaptation of Kenneth Grahame's *Wind in the Willows*. In this I had a leading role, that of Badger. Robin Barriball was a hilarious Toad, Frank Delfos was Mole and Gordon was Ratty. The part of the judge was played by Michael Hulme, a boy who was often ridiculed by other students, although he was quite brilliant in the part. He had to eat sandwiches while sitting on the judge's bench. I am ashamed to say that we very nastily added boot polish to the sandwich filling. Michael, however, proved to be a real trooper and ate the sandwiches without flinching. I never heard that he was ill afterwards, but he did gain greater respect from all of us.

Every year the nearby town of Selukwe held an eisteddfod. Several of us were entered for various categories, including playing the piano, singing and poetry recitation. The first time I entered, I sang Schubert's 'Who is Sylvia?' (words by Shakespeare) and scored the top marks in my age group. At the end of the eisteddfod week all the winners were invited to perform in a concert in Selukwe's hall. This meant that we actually left the school campus on a Saturday night, which was a great occasion. Unfortunately, when it came to my turn to sing at the concert, I started singing off key. The accompanist stopped playing, but I soldiered on until the end of the song. What an embarrassment!

At the end of my fourth year at Guinea Fowl, Douglas Ferrer, the founding headmaster, retired. Much to my surprise, my father was invited to give the farewell speech on behalf of the parents. Why he was asked I don't know. Since Guinea Fowl was a boarding school, parents had very little involvement and there was no PTA. Perhaps it was because Dad was a friendly, outgoing person who would stop and chat to teachers and other parents whenever he picked me up from the school. Pupils were not invited to this farewell event, but I learnt that Dad had made an excellent speech, a copy of which I was later able to read. I was very proud of him.

School holidays were divided between Umvuma with Dad and Bulawayo with Mom. Although I was always happy to see Mom, I hated spending time under the same roof as my stepfather, Uncle Monty.

In December 1952, I sat the Cambridge School Certificate, the equivalent of today's GCSE exams. When the results came out I had passed, with distinctions in Latin and – surprisingly – Afrikaans, and just missed a distinction in mathematics. I got credits in the rest of the subjects except two: Religious Knowledge (which I was not required to take and expected to fail) and Geography (which I passed but did not achieve a 'credit' grade). I was never much good at Geography. Mr Jack Court, the Geography teacher, always said that my essays read more like travelogues than serious geography. Physical geography just never appealed to me, though I knew the names of nearly every capital city in the world! Jack Court, incidentally, called all the girls by their surnames. It was normal practice at Guinea Fowl for boys to be called only by their surnames, but girls were addressed by their first names. Jack Court was the exception.

Now I was in the sixth form and had to choose my Higher School Certificate subjects, two at higher level and two at subsidiary level. I chose Latin and Mathematics at higher level, and – if I remember correctly – English and History at subsidiary level. I started on my Higher School Certificate in 1953. I also became a house prefect. This was something I did not enjoy, though I liked the perks that came with the job, especially having a private study instead of having to attend 'prep' every evening. But by this time I had become rather bored with school. My enthusiasm seemed to have disappeared. Whether it was the isolation of Guinea Fowl or the dismal prospect of two more years of school, I had begun to feel the need for a new challenge and more excitement. I wanted to get on with my life.

Rhodes

There was a system whereby, if you obtained five 'credits' in certain subjects at School Certificate level, you achieved what was called Matriculation Exemption, which meant in theory you could gain entry directly to a South African university. It was not a route used by many pupils in Rhodesia – most stayed on to complete the two-year Higher School Certificate. I begged and begged my father to see whether he could get me into university straight away. He contacted Rhodes University in Grahamstown (which was the university I wanted to attend). Lo and behold, they accepted me! I arrived at Rhodes a couple of weeks after the start of their term (which only began in mid-February). I was, in fact, the first boy from Guinea Fowl to attend university. (One of the girls, Juliette Phillips, a talented pianist, had gone to Cape Town University a year earlier.) I was also the first member of my extended family to go to university.

When I left Guinea Fowl, my fellow sixth-formers presented me with two books: *Whitaker's Almanack* and *The Liberation of Mankind* by Willem Henrik van Loon. Rather strange, but perhaps appropriate choices – probably selected by our form teacher, George Turnbull. I treasure them still.

At sixteen I was too young to attend university and always felt out of place, particularly during that first year. First-year students at Rhodes were known as 'inks'. The origin of the word is still disputed. Some say it refers to inky school children, others that it comes from a Xhosa word meaning 'nothing'. In any case, inks were regarded as the lowest of the low. A senior student could stand in the middle of the quadrangle in our residence and shout, "Ink". Any ink within earshot was required to come running and do whatever the senior wanted. If I remember correctly, this system of fagging lasted for only the first six weeks. Most senior students did not abuse their position, but there were always a few who did. One student in particular, whose name I have forgotten, used to return to the house nearly every night totally drunk, but sober enough to shout, "Ink". We would have to carry him to his room and sometimes clean up his vomit.

I was assigned to Botha House, one of the oldest residences at Rhodes. Each student was allocated a single room. I was lucky enough to be given a corner room, which had a double aspect and was somewhat larger than other rooms.

Since childhood I had always wanted to become a criminal lawyer – an 'advocate' in South Africa, a barrister in the UK. I had read several books about famous lawyers, including a thrilling biography of Sir Patrick Hastings and a book about Clarence Darrow, and I fancied myself in such roles. Although Dad supported my ambition, my stepfather (my mother's husband whom I called Uncle Monty) was opposed, believing that only a career in business was worthwhile. So I compromised and began studying for a B.Com (Law). In the first year, in addition to Latin and English, this meant studying Economics/Economic History and Accounting. These last two subjects I did not enjoy.

Together with a number of other students, I volunteered to teach mathematics a couple of evenings a week in a school for black children and adults in Grahamstown. And I discovered that I really loved teaching and had a talent for it. It was a very rewarding experience. The students varied in age from late teens to middle age, but they were tremendously motivated. Most had day jobs, and because their homes in the black township had no electricity, they did their homework under streetlights! I greatly admired their resolve and endurance.

This experience convinced me that teaching was my vocation, and this certainty remained with me throughout my working life. Of course, I could not foresee how my future career would develop, nor had I any clear philosophical ideas on education, but I have never regretted my decision to become a teacher.

I have written elsewhere about the consternation this decision caused to my stepfather. Persuading Dad was quite easy, but Uncle Monty was totally set against the idea. But I went ahead anyway. It also had academic consequences: in order not to lose a year I was virtually obliged to major in Latin and English, since these were the only 'teaching' subjects I had taken in my first year.

One advantage of choosing teaching as a career was that the Rhodesian government took over the payment of my tuition fees and living expenses. (In return I was contracted to serve at least two years as a teacher in a state school.) Since Dad was in financial trouble and Uncle Monty was totally opposed to my even being at university, this was a real boon and gave me a certain independence I would not otherwise have had.

So my B.Com course was converted into a B.A. course, and English and Latin became my major subjects virtually by default.

In my second year I added Beginners' Greek, mathematics and Shona (the main African language spoken in Rhodesia) to my course list. In all of these I just managed to scrape a pass. Although mathematics had been my strongest subject at school, I had taken it only to School Certificate level, which was not really high enough for university studies. In my final year, I studied just my two major subjects and got a third in English and a second in Latin. So academically, my first degree was not very distinguished.

The best student in the Latin class at Rhodes was a brilliant but highly-strung girl named Ann Esser. In the final examination Ann was expected by everyone to gain a first. During the exam, however, she dropped her pen, and bent down to pick it up. The invigilator, perhaps relishing his power, shouted at her, virtually accusing her of trying to cheat. Ann just collapsed and had to leave the hall without finishing the exam. She was later granted an 'aegrotat', but I am not sure whether she obtained the first that she so richly deserved.

I found life at university stimulating and exciting, especially from the beginning of my second year, when my friends from Guinea Fowl School joined me at Rhodes. Barry van Blomestein, Gordon Phillips and John Kemp, all among my closest friends at boarding school, had chosen Rhodes University. This completely changed my social life. In my first year I had struggled as the youngest student at the university, arriving three weeks after the start of the academic year. Although I got on well with other students, my chronic shyness rather stood in the way of my social integration.

Whereas at school I had always been among the highest-performing students, at Rhodes my performance was mediocre. This was partly due no doubt to my coming to university before I was ready, partly to my actual ability, but mainly due to the fact that I did not really work very hard at Rhodes, doing the bare minimum to get by.

I was quite active in various societies, running the economics society (why, I don't know, since the subject did not excite me, but we did get a number of interesting speakers for our meetings). I also participated in debates and in drama.

In a production of *Macbeth* I played the part of Menteith who has about seventy words in the whole play. *Macbeth* is, of course, one of Shakespeare's greatest tragedies, but we had the audience rolling in the aisles with laughter. The set consisted of enormous, tall half-cylinders which were meant to be moved around throughout the production into different formations. But the cylinders were so heavy that nearly all the cast had to come on stage each time to push them around. It was hilarious.

I also took part in a production of *For Better for Worse*, a light comedy. This was put on by the Grahamstown Amateur Dramatic Society, and in it I played the lead as a young, newly married man.

This was far more successful. Interestingly, the man who played my father-in-law was John Paterson, whom I met many years later when he was head of the Commonwealth-American School of Lausanne and I was head of the Lycée des Nations International School in Geneva. (John, who is now dead, later became chairman of the European Council of International Schools.)

On one occasion, I was approached by a student who was studying drama and wanted me to act as a model for a make-up demonstration he was giving. He said I had an ideal face for this. I was rather flattered and so agreed. Much to my chagrin he made me up as Mephistopheles! Because the make-up paint was luminous I decided to play a trick on Rudolf Gruber, a good friend of mine. I knocked on his door, and when he opened it he thought I was the devil. He became very agitated and grabbed a wooden bat from his cupboard and raised it to strike me. I only just managed to persuade him that I was the person behind the Mephistophelian mask. In later years, despite losing his sight, Dolf became Director of the South Africa Foundation in Germany.

Playing sport was never my strong suit, but for a couple of years John Kemp and I used to meet before breakfast nearly every day to play either tennis or squash. If only I had kept this up after leaving university! On one occasion I played cricket for the 'social thirds', as the lowest cricket team was known. Batting low down the order, I managed to play defensively for nearly half an hour (making an undefeated eight runs), thus allowing my batting partner to take us to victory. That was the highlight of my cricketing career.

Hitchhiking was something we did often, sometimes to Port Elizabeth (PE), once even to Johannesburg, about 800 miles from Grahamstown. It did not seem to be a dangerous way to travel then.

During one Easter vacation, a friend, Steyn Maartens, gave me a lift on the back of his motorbike all the way to Johannesburg and back. We went there to see the Rand Easter Show. Much to my dismay, I bumped into my stepfather there – he had come down from Bulawayo with my mother to visit the show. Needless to say he was not amused that I had travelled so far on the back of a motorbike. Steyn, however, was an excellent motorcyclist, though in those days nobody wore crash helmets, just a pair of sunglasses. Sadly, the year after he left university, he was knocked over by a lorry and killed. A great loss, for he was a brilliant student and a good friend.

University vacations were still shared between Mom in Bulawayo and Dad in Umvuma. In addition to the Falcon Hotel, Dad had recklessly bought a farm about ten miles from Umvuma. This was a grave business error. He had saddled himself with a huge mortgage and still had to run the hotel. It is not surprising that within a couple of years he was overwhelmed by debt and was declared bankrupt.

Dad was someone who became enthusiastic about projects and excited by new ideas (a characteristic that I share). His enthusiasm sometimes impaired his judgment. Buying a farm was one such misjudgment.

The farm had come onto the market when one of his clients at the Falcon Hotel decided to sell.

I can understand why Dad and Stella fell in love with the farm. It was a beautiful place. Part of it was forested with eucalyptus trees with a working sawmill attached. The main crop was tobacco, a thriving industry in Rhodesia at the time.

Above all, there was a lovely farmhouse. Dad and Stella had lived so long in a wood and iron shack with an outside toilet. How they must have longed for a real home. Here was the opportunity: a thriving farm and sawmill, which should produce sufficient income to cover the enormous mortgage they took on.

Alas, they knew nothing about farming. Tobacco, in particular, once picked, needed careful drying in the barns where the temperature had to be constantly monitored and controlled. The weather that year did not favour them either. They had no financial cushion and were eventually forced to sell both the hotel and the farm.

For Gail, Barbi and me, the farm was a wonderful place. We ate corn grown in our garden lashed with freshly churned butter from the dairy. In our garden I came face to face with a black mamba, a terrifying encounter. A farmhand who was nearby quickly dispatched it using a gardening fork and a spade.

There, Dad taught me to drive, and at the age of seventeen, so lax were the local regulations, I drove myself from the farm to Umvuma's police station to undergo my driving test. The test, conducted by the local policeman, consisted of a short drive around Umvuma (there was scarcely any traffic) and some manoeuvring around a series of empty oil drums in the police car park. (Some years later, when teaching at Churchill School, I took my heavy-vehicle driving test, as we used to ferry our sports teams all over the country in an open lorry. To pass the test I drove the lorry through the streets of Salisbury. At the end of the test I passed, having been told, "Nobody ever learns to drive a truck properly until they have been given a chance to drive one. So I am giving you your licence!") Just to prove that my licence was really valid, I subsequently also passed the Institute of Advanced Motorists test.

To travel from Grahamstown to Bulawayo by train was a major journey. It took three days and two nights. Since there was no direct train line from South Africa to Rhodesia, we had to pass through Botswana (then called Bechuanaland). At one point we were asked to get off the train in order to lighten the load and enable the train, pulled by two engines, to climb a steep gradient. The train would sometimes arrive in Bulawayo a whole day late, meaning that we had to spend an extra night on the train. Continuing the journey to Salisbury meant changing trains in Bulawayo and spending yet another night on board. Since the trains were steam trains we were filthy from the coal soot and dust. The only washing facility was a small basin in the compartment that doubled as a table. The seats in the second-class compartments converted into six bunk beds, and each passenger was given a roll of bedding to use.

Following my undistinguished B.A. degree, I stayed on for a year of teacher training. This qualification was known as a University Education Diploma or UED. Apart from Helen Coppen, an audiovisual enthusiast, the lecturers in the education department were singularly uninspiring. But the course did give me a chance to read widely on educational philosophy and innovative teaching methods.

During my UED course I was lucky enough to be asked to stand in for a few weeks for the regular Latin teacher at St Andrew's School in Grahamstown. This was (and still is) one of the leading schools in South Africa. My three weeks there were a great experience and stood me in good stead once I started my teaching career.

Although the UED took place during my fourth year at Rhodes, students destined for a teaching career were expected to do 'practice' teaching during the university winter holidays in July. I was assigned to Milton School in Bulawayo during my second and third years. Bear in mind that I was younger than some of the pupils at the school. In order to carry out my practice teaching, I wore corduroy trousers, a sports jacket and tie. On one occasion a young first-year pupil (aged about twelve) came up to me and pulled my tie. "Our head boy says we have to wear a school tie and blazer," he said. I am not sure which of us was more embarrassed when I explained that I was a teacher.

Teaching in Rhodesia

As the recipient of a teacher-training grant, I was obliged, as stated earlier, to teach for a minimum of two years. I could also be sent to a school anywhere in Southern Rhodesia. I expressed a preference for a post in Salisbury (now Harare), the capital of Southern Rhodesia. I was delighted, therefore, when I was appointed to teach Latin at Churchill School, a newish boys' high school located in Eastlea, a suburb of Salisbury.

A few days before the start of the new school year, in January 1957, I put on my only suit and went to see the school's imposing headmaster, E J Hougaard, who had a rather fearsome reputation. 'Jeeves', as he was known behind his back, was an intimidating figure. He was determined to make his school the country's leading school. He insisted that all boys should wear school uniform, not only in the school, but also in any public place. Any boy found in a shop not wearing the proper uniform (including a school cap and regulation socks) would be hauled before the headmaster the next day and beaten (usually two 'cuts' or strokes of the cane on the buttocks).

Needless to say, I was very nervous at my interview. He gave me a short pep talk about the standards of behaviour expected at the school, then dismissed me, saying, "I like the look of you. You'll make a good schoolmaster." I was walking on air when I left his office.

Mr Hougaard lived up to his reputation. Although very strict, he always tried to be fair and was willing to listen to any ideas put to him. When he was appointed to the school it was known as Eastlea Boys' High School. He personally wrote to Winston Churchill to ask his permission to name the school Churchill School. The boarding house was named Winston House, and the school's sports houses were named after Battle of Britain pilots. To distinguish the school from others in the country, he established a pipe band, which developed an excellent reputation and played several times in Scotland itself.

The school was an ugly two-storied concrete building, forming three sides of a quadrangle. For school assemblies we all gathered in the quadrangle. Mr Hougaard stood on the walkway outside his office on the upper floor and addressed us from there. (Later, I would think of John Cleese in *Clockwise*.)

One boy who was caught smoking was made to sit all morning on a chair in the quadrangle and forced to smoke. Such public humiliation was not uncommon, though a few strokes of the cane was a more usual punishment.

When Professor Rousseau, head of the education department at the new University College of Rhodesia and Nyasaland (then a constituent college of the University of London), visited Churchill School with a group of his students, they went into Mr Hougaard's office. Professor Rousseau asked Hougaard to explain his philosophy of education. Hougaard walked over to the cupboard, pulled out a selection of canes, and said, "This is my philosophy of education." The students were quickly ushered out of the office by a crestfallen Professor Rousseau.

I was made head of the Latin department; in fact, I was the Latin department, but the position carried a small allowance of £50 a year. I was determined to make use of the direct method of teaching Latin that I had read about during my teacher-training course. Excited by the possibility, I subscribed to the Linguaphone Latin Course, which disappointingly consisted of just a couple of records on which the great WHD Rouse provided a few examples of his methodology. Undaunted, I nevertheless used his method for the early stages of teaching Latin. English was banned from the classroom, declensions and conjugations were thrown out of the window, and instead we used only Latin.

Unfortunately, I could not actually speak Latin; like most Latin teachers I had a good reading knowledge of the language, but had never had the opportunity to speak it. Nevertheless, I persevered, switching to English explanations only after several months. Even then, I eschewed the traditional teaching methods of mensa, mensa, mensam (table, o table, table) and amo, amas, amat, using instead the excellent teaching course designed by the Perse School, Cambridge.

I became a member of the Association for the Reform of Latin Teaching and the Joint Association of Classical Teachers. When the Cambridge Latin Course (much influenced by these organisations and now widely used) was first published, I was among its first and most enthusiastic adherents. I always felt that teaching and learning had to be fun and had to involve all the senses. Despite my comparatively unorthodox methods, regarded sceptically by many colleagues, the results obtained by my students were among the best in the country.

Because my teaching methods were regarded as both avant-garde and successful, I was recruited by the University College of Rhodesia and Nyasaland as a part-time lecturer in the teaching of Latin in the Department of Education, a position I held until I left Rhodesia.

Professor Carney, the dynamic Head of the Department of Classics at UCRN, established the African Classical Association and invited a number of teachers, including myself, to join the governing body. We organised conferences and activities for students throughout the city and beyond. The Proceedings of the African Classical Association became a respectable academic journal to which I contributed.

My involvement in the life of Churchill School was absolute. I ran the debating society, establishing a countrywide schools' debating tournament, persuading our local MP, Peter Schaub, to provide a trophy for the winner. I set up a Music Appreciation Society, held on Sunday evenings, to which a significant number of boys came and where they first tasted classical music. (Providing cakes and Cokes acted as a huge incentive, especially to the boarders.)

Together with my great friend Willie Marais (who alas died of a heart attack in his mid-thirties), we put on several musical productions: *Trial by Jury* and *Patience* by Gilbert and Sullivan, and the twelve-year-old Mozart's opera *Bastien et Bastienne*. The Mozart piece did not go down well, but the two Gilbert and Sullivan operas were very well received. Willie directed the productions and I was the musical director even though I could barely pick out a tune on the piano.

Since Churchill was a boys' school, all the female parts were sung by boys. In a school with no musical tradition, it was almost impossible to find enough boys willing to sing. However, Willie and I managed to persuade the captain of the first rugby team, together with several of his teammates, to join the chorus. This immediately changed the views of the rest of the school and we were bombarded with offers to take part.

Patience was a big production, for which we gathered together a twenty-piece semi-professional orchestra. (Most of the musicians played in the Salisbury Symphony Orchestra.) As the musical director, I was expected to conduct the orchestra. My only knowledge of conducting was derived from a recording I had of Bruno Walter conducting a rehearsal of Mozart's 'Linz' symphony. You could hear him stopping the orchestra periodically to make a comment on their performance.

At our first orchestra rehearsal, I had no idea how to start. When I raised my baton the orchestra seemed to ignore me. I knew nothing of upbeats and downbeats. I tried to use some of Bruno Walter's phrases, such as asking the violins to sing a little more. It was a total disaster and the members of the orchestra were ready to walk out. I begged them to give me one more week to sort myself out.

The next day, I approached Eileen Reynolds, Principal of the Rhodesian Academy of Music, and asked for her help. She was a formidable character, but was intrigued, amused and challenged by my dilemma. So she set about teaching me to conduct. Every evening, I spent a couple of hours with her. We would play my recording of *Patience*, conducted by Sir Malcolm Sargent, and I would conduct it in front of Eileen Reynolds. She was a brilliant teacher and by the time of our next orchestra rehearsal, I confidently led the orchestra through the score.

All teachers at Churchill were expected to coach a sport. In my first year, I was given the Under 14B cricket team, a job which I loved. They did well, and I was rewarded the next year by being assigned to the Under 13A team, the top team of first-year pupils. Every Saturday during the cricket season, we had a match against another school. I was fortunate in having a number of very talented players, several of whom went on to play cricket for Rhodesia. The most brilliant was Stuart Robertson, an outstanding batsman and wicketkeeper. (Just recently, thanks to Facebook, I was contacted by one of my former pupils, Alastair Grierson-Rickford, who played for my team. He had retired from his job as a teacher at Felsted School and invited me to Lord's, where he is a member. He has just published a superb book on the history of Felsted School.)

Unfortunately, cricket was not played during the winter term, when rugby was king. I hated rugby, but nevertheless was given a lowly junior team to coach. Since I was ignorant of the rules of the game, my team fared pretty badly. After one term of coaching rugby I was assigned to tennis, a sport that was regarded as peripheral and unimportant, but I relished my new assignment.

In my first couple of years, I lived in digs in the house of an elderly couple, the Windsors. (I say elderly, but they were probably younger than I am now!) They provided all my meals (including delicious pancakes on Fridays), cleaning and laundry, all for £18 a month. I bought a bicycle and used to cycle to work. At the end of my first year of teaching I bought my first car, a used (very used) Morris Minor, which I lovingly cleaned and polished every week.

After about a year, the Windsors decided that they wanted my room for other purposes and I was obliged to seek other accommodation. I was lucky to find a room in the house of a delightful young couple, the Charltons, who had a baby. I used to hold a weekly evening class in my room for my sixth-form students who were studying Latin for A Level. We would listen to the *Goon Show*, a uniquely crazy radio comedy with Harry Secombe, Spike Milligan and Peter Sellers, before getting down to the serious study of Vergil and Cicero. Mrs Charlton used to supply us with tea and biscuits.

Although Churchill was mainly a day school, there was a boarding house for about sixty pupils. Winston House was an unprepossessing place, a one-storey building forming a quadrangle, with three dormitories, each housing twenty boys. In the corners were two rooms for teachers and alongside was the headmaster's house. After a couple of years, I became a non-resident duty master at Winston House and then managed to persuade Jeeves to convert an outbuilding into a bedroom so that I could become resident.

While it was convenient to live on the premises, the duties were pretty onerous. My fellow duty masters were Ken Cripwell, a dynamic English teacher who later became a lecturer at the University of London Institute of Education, and Paul Hjul, who was in charge of history and who became my closest friend. Both Paul and Ken died young. I seem to have had a knack of losing my close friends, for, in addition to Paul and Ken, Willie Marais, Gordon Phillips, Steyn Maartens, Barry van Blomestein and Nicki Bennett all died before their time.

The food at Winston House was slightly better than at Guinea Fowl School, which I had attended as a boy. The matron and cook, Mrs Bands, did her best. It was not always clear what we were eating, so we referred to her stews as LPMs, Little Pieces of Meat.

While relations with the boarders were quite friendly, disciplinary offences were dealt with in only one way: corporal punishment. I did not like it, but did not know any other way. One day, a student, quite a senior boy whose behaviour was often erratic, absolutely refused to bend over to receive his punishment. This had never happened to me before and I was nonplussed. How should I deal with this insubordination? I invited the student to sit down to chat about it. He told me of his humiliation at being punished in this way. To me, this was a revelation and I undertook never to beat him or any other pupil again. He became my greatest ally in the boarding house, often quelling trouble before I intervened. Discipline and behaviour improved and I have never administered corporal punishment since.

Indeed, in education, I am not a great believer in punishment. Sometimes it is necessary, if only to demonstrate support for the victim in cases such as bullying. But I don't think it helps to alter the behaviour of the perpetrator. Far more effective is leading a child to see that what he or she has done is wrong.

Teachers in Rhodesia were entitled to one term's leave after two years and one term. If you did not take your leave, it accumulated up to a maximum of two terms. It was then possible, subject to approval, to add a further term's unpaid leave so that you could have a whole year's sabbatical in order to undertake further studies. So in 1961 I was granted a year's leave in order to take an Honours degree in Latin. (In South Africa at the time, an Honours degree was a postgraduate degree taken after the award of a first Bachelor's degree.)

I decided to take my Honours degree at the University of the Witwatersrand ('Wits') in Johannesburg. As luck would have it, the professor of Classics was himself on a sabbatical that year. His place was taken by Professor T J Haarhoff, Emeritus Professor from Cape Town University and regarded by all as South Africa's most distinguished classical scholar. This was a great opportunity for me to study with an exceptional classicist and a fine teacher. I managed to graduate with first-class Honours and was awarded the Hellenic Community Prize as the best student in the Department of Classics. Professor Haarhoff told me that my prose composition (this is what they call translation into Latin) was the best he had ever seen in an examination. I believe it was my four years of teaching Latin that had effected this improvement in my technique.

During my year at Wits I lived with a couple who were down on their luck but owned a beautiful and enormous house in Westcliff, a posh suburb close to the university. They had two daughters in their twenties as well as several other lodgers. It was a chaotic household, completely disorganised. Mealtimes were frantic affairs and nearly always ended in a slanging match between the daughters and their parents. But we had fun, too, and I enjoyed staying there.

One of the lodgers, aged about twenty, claimed that he was an art student. Every day he would leave the house ostensibly to go to college, but it turned out that he simply used to wander around and spent most of his time at the movies (or bioscope, as we used to call the cinema). When he finally left the house for non-payment of rent, they found dozens of chicken bones under his mattress.

Although lonely at first, I enjoyed my time in Jo'burg. The buzz and dynamism of the big city really appealed to me. Strangely, I never felt threatened or intimidated there, but I understand that it has now become a violent place with a high murder rate. More recently, steps have been taken to change this. I hope they will be successful.

Coincidentally, my year at Wits coincided with my father's lowest point financially. He had been made bankrupt and was in desperate financial straits. He and Stella moved to a cheap hotel in Johannesburg. Dad got a job as a travelling shoe salesman on commission. Although outwardly cheerful, I know that he was deeply upset by the failure of his business, losing both the hotel in Umvuma and the farm he had so unwisely purchased a few years before.

Fortunately, Dad was an excellent hotelier and soon afterwards became manager of the Wilderness Hotel, a beautiful hotel on the Garden Route between Port Elizabeth and Cape Town. I understand that he expunged his bankruptcy by paying off all his debts.

On my return to Churchill School, three of us on the staff – Willie Marais, Martin Sinclair (the last I heard of him he was deputy head of a large comprehensive school in South London) and I – rented a three-bedroomed house close to the school. It was great having our own place. Everything in the house was taken care of by our African servant, Famba, who lived in a reasonably comfortable outbuilding in the garden. It shocks me now to think how easily we slipped into a master-servant relationship. Yet I am comforted by the knowledge that we always treated Famba with respect and just let him get on with the job.

I also resumed my lecturing at the University College of Rhodesia and Nyasaland. One of my students in the course was Doreen Herzstein, a mature student who had decided late in life to become a teacher. She and her husband became great friends and welcomed me into their home. They had three delightful children and all of them made me feel that I was part of their family. They also introduced me to my first serious girlfriend, Sheila Flower (not her real name). Her father owned a butcher shop in Salisbury. One day I was standing in his shop waiting for Sheila when a large rat ran across the floor. Somehow I could not get this image of the rat together with Sheila out of my mind. Unjustly, I quickly ended my courtship.

Saturday nights were usually spent at the home of Bill Bennett (in charge of modern languages at Churchill) and his feisty French wife, Nicki. Television had just been introduced in Rhodesia and we would all gather round Bill and Nicki's TV set to watch *Dr Kildare*. Nicki was a wonderful cook and always produced the most tasty snacks. A few years later, after I had left Rhodesia, I heard that she had died.

One evening, a few of us were invited to dinner by a young French teacher and his wife. This was the first dinner party they had given. The wife, who had very little experience in the kitchen, decided to cook a chicken, simply boiled. It was quite normal in those days to buy a chicken that had not yet been plucked or eviscerated. She had got rid of most of the feathers, but had not removed and cleaned the bird's innards before cooking. When the chicken arrived at the table the smell was terrible. She was so upset and embarrassed, but we all laughed it off and had a great evening in any case.

At that time, Southern Rhodesia, Northern Rhodesia and Nyasaland were joined as the Federation of Rhodesia and Nyasaland. African nationalists were beginning to put pressure on the British government to break up the Federation and grant independence to Nyasaland and Northern Rhodesia. Dr Hastings Banda, leader of the African nationalist party in Nyasaland, was particularly vocal, while in Northern Rhodesia, Dr Kenneth Kaunda led the protests. In 1963, the British government capitulated and agreed to the break-up of the Federation, leading to the establishment of Malawi (Nyasaland) and Zambia (Northern Rhodesia). Southern Rhodesia would become Rhodesia and remain a self-governing colony.

On the dissolution of the Federation, teachers were offered a number of choices: they could opt to teach in any of the three countries and their pensions would be protected, or they could resign from the teaching service and receive what was called a 'golden handshake'. (The word 'golden' was an exaggeration. I was offered approximately £2000, which amounted to about a year's salary.)

Coming to a decision was difficult. Politically, it was an exciting time. Rhodesia's Prime Minister was Garfield Todd, originally from New Zealand. He was liberal in his views, believed in equality, and if not universal suffrage, at least one in which race was not a qualification. He also wanted to repeal the act which divided the land into racial areas. I was a strong supporter of Garfield Todd, but it was clear that his liberal views were not acceptable to the majority of the mainly white electorate. Should I stay in Rhodesia or should I leave? I changed my mind several times before I decided that I would take my golden handshake and travel to Europe to study. My plans were vague, but I particularly wanted to learn Italian. My classical studies had made me eager to get to know Italy, of which I had romantic notions. The previous year I had been offered an Italian government scholarship to study in Italy, but was not able to accept it at the time.

I booked a cheap berth on the SS *Europa*, operated by the Lloyd Triestino Line, sailing up the east coast of Africa with an all-Italian crew.

Before embarking, I stopped off to visit Dad and family in Britstown where he was now running an excellent hotel in the middle of the Karoo. It was a popular stopping-off place for those travelling by car from Johannesburg to Cape Town. Here is an extract from my diary written on Boxing Day 1963:

"Another hot, scorching day, with barely air to breathe. Surely Britstown must be one of the hottest, remotest, most desolate and derelict towns on earth. Yet the hotel seems to be a goldmine. It was completely packed tonight.

"There's a delightful old permanent here, Mr Glazer. He's been in Britstown for 'a hoenderd and tventy yeers' and speaks an engaging mixture of English, Afrikaans and Yiddish.

"Pleasantest memories of Britstown: the long walks late at night, usually with my father. It is only at night that there is time to talk, and this we do as we stroll around the deserted streets, and later as Dad has his 11 p.m. tea and sandwiches in lieu of supper."

Next stop was Port Elizabeth to which I travelled in a filthy overnight train from De Aar. There, I was met by Mom, Uncle Monty and Vicki and we spent two weeks in their caravan. (I've never enjoyed caravanning or camping!)

At last I boarded the ship at Port Elizabeth with an enormous silver-coloured tin trunk in which were packed all my possessions including scores of books. In retrospect I was clearly not a seasoned traveller, not anticipating that I would have to drag this heavy trunk all over Europe. I shared a cramped bunk-bedded cabin with three other young guys. There were also many other young people of my age on board, both male and female. So the whole trip was very lively and a lot of fun.

Outside the cabin, the ship was quite luxurious and the food was excellent. I asked to sit at a table with Italian-speakers in the hope that I would learn a little Italian en route.

Our first stop was East London, then Durban. I happened to keep a diary for this part of the journey, and this is what I wrote at the time: "The city is greatly changed since last I saw it in 1950, but I found it dull until I came into the Indian quarter. I was hoping to have a curry at The Nest, but apparently it is no more. So I asked an Indian where I could eat curry, and he directed me to the Delhi restaurant, which proved to be a dingy non-white establishment where they were not permitted to serve me. However, they in turn sent me to the Victory Lounge, an even dingier place (also for non-whites) where they were not so fussy. I was so enchanted by this section of the town that I had lunch there, although as soon as I saw it I felt quite ill, as the place really wasn't very clean. However, I didn't want to give offence and so ate most of the curry. It was quite tasty and, if served better, would have been enjoyable. I'm afraid I am still too squeamish to enjoy food in a smelly, dirty place. But still, it was an interesting experience.

"After lunch I stumbled on the Indian Market – a fascinating place, particularly the people. The Indians, I think, are physically the most handsome race I know, especially when they are young. The women are lovely and the men handsome. There is an Indian couple on board, and the woman is quite enchantingly beautiful." A prescient remark, as I was later to fall in love with and marry a beautiful Indian woman myself.

Once we reached Beira, Mozambique's main port, I felt that my travels had really begun.

The ship was due to call at Dar-es-Salaam and Zanzibar, but there was a military coup in progress (which resulted in Tanganyika and Zanzibar becoming Tanzania). So we sailed past these and stopped at Mombasa in Kenya. From the moment we first saw the harbour, I knew I would like the place. The first impression was beautiful: thick vegetation, palm trees, bougainvillea, hibiscus, and miles of pure white beaches. The town itself fascinated me: such a mingling of races and tongues, such a contrast of old and new, Arabs, Europeans, Africans and Indians. During our stop there we visited the fabulous Nyali beach. Five of us hired a car at 1/- a mile, and in the evening we visited a nightclub and were amazed to see white and black people dancing together both on the floor and in the cabaret. For someone brought up in Southern Africa, this was a salutary shock to the system.

The scheduled stop in Mogadishu, Somalia, was also cancelled because of political trouble. So our next port of call was Aden, which surprised me by its beautiful setting, surrounded by dramatic mountains. Aden was a duty-free port and all passengers would stock up on the latest technology. I bought a Rodania watch and a portable record player (as if I did not already have more than enough luggage to drag around).

Next stop: Suez, where we disembarked to catch a bus to Cairo while the *SS Europa* made its way through the Suez Canal.

Cairo was a throbbing, vibrant city. Of course, the Pyramids and the Sphinx were essential viewing and a camel ride obligatory, but I was struck by the beauty of the Nile and overwhelmed by the treasures in the Cairo museum.

Europe at Last

At last we were on our way to Europe. After a couple of days at sea we had crossed the Mediterranean, stopping briefly in Brindisi. When we went to bed that night we knew that our three-week voyage would end the next day in Venice. As we emerged from our cabin for breakfast that morning we were greeted by the most magnificent sight I had ever seen. It was mid-February and dawn was just breaking over the city. The approach to Venice by sea, with the dawn light reflecting from its splendid buildings and shimmering canals, was something I will never forget. The word awesome was invented for this sight.

Four of us, three girls and myself, together with my tin trunk, shared a room that night in a cheap pensione. (Nothing happened!) We also saw a rather threadbare production of Mozart's *The Abduction from the Seraglio* at La Fenice, Venice's ornate opera house. (Years later, La Fenice burnt down, but has now been lovingly restored, as my wife Marj and I saw on a recent visit to Venice.)

After exploring Venice we went our separate ways. I took the train to Milan, Florence, Rome and Naples, stopping for a few days in each of these cities. In each place I attended the opera and went on tours. It was an exhilarating experience; Naples has an incomparable setting and some lovely architecture. The San Carlo opera house is a rival in splendour to La Scala in Milan. And, of course, Naples has the ruins of Pompeii and Herculaneum, which were very exciting to someone interested in Roman history. The Archaeological Museum in Naples has so many fascinating artefacts. Yet a drive around the city also revealed appalling poverty, many people still living at that time in the ruins of buildings destroyed during the Second World War nearly twenty years after its conclusion. Also in Naples, I was pickpocketed while travelling on a tram, the only time this has happened to me – so far.

My incongruous tin trunk had been sent by rail to Rome, but when I returned to Rome station it was nowhere to be found. Struggling in Italian, I eventually persuaded a member of the station staff to let me look for it myself. He took me to an enormous warehouse large enough to swallow up the Royal Albert Hall. It was full of cases, trunks, parcels, prams, bicycles and other sundry items. Feeling totally helpless and convinced that I would never see my beloved books again, I walked up and down the rows of goods for what seemed like hours. Lo and behold, at last I found my trunk and was able to reclaim it.

I could not get over the magnificence of Rome. All the places and events that I had studied came to life as I explored it. It remains my favourite city. I returned to it several times during my stay in Italy, each time experiencing something new. In the summer I attended a thrilling performance of *Aida* in the Baths of Caracalla.

It was now time to begin my study of Italian, and I decided to do so in Florence at the *Centro di Cultura*. Having settled into a pensione nearby, I attended classes for nearly a month. The teaching was awful. We were given no opportunity to speak Italian. Instead we were simply expected to learn the grammar from a textbook.

I decided to look elsewhere. I had heard of the *Università italiana per stranieri* in Perugia and decided to enrol there. The course there was even worse than that in Florence. There must have been more than a hundred students in the class. The *professoressa* sat at a desk in front of the class, barely visible to those near the back. She would read from a textbook, seldom look at the students and never involve us in the lesson. Her teaching was quite the worst I have ever come across.

Because I loved Perugia, I decided to remain there for another two months. I had a beautiful room in a large comfortable house. We used to have meals in the apartment of a woman who lived across the road. One of her diners was a very elegant young woman who claimed to be an Indian princess, the daughter of a maharajah. The *principessa*, as our hostess always addressed her, was supposed to be learning Italian, but made absolutely no attempt whatsoever to do so.

Fed up with the slow progress of my Italian class, I decided instead to learn French. I had read of the audiovisual teaching methods supported by the French government for the teaching of French to foreigners. So I enrolled in a course at the University of Besançon. What a contrast with the feeble teaching in Italy. Here, we were drilled for five hours a day. All the teaching at the start was oral – in other words we learnt to speak before we read or wrote. A couple of hours each day were spent in the language lab where we could practise the new patterns we had learnt in the morning. At the same time as our course, French students were studying English at the university. We shared recreational facilities and had many opportunities to practise our French while the French students also practised their English. It was an enlightened arrangement, which benefited us all. A Bulgarian girl, who could speak neither French nor English, became remarkably fluent in both languages by the end of the course!

I became very good friends with Michel Lapointe who invited me to visit him and his family in Nevers, where I spent a very enjoyable few days. Their house had no bathroom (we used the kitchen sink to wash ourselves) and only an outside toilet. It was so cold in my bedroom that I needed to go to the loo several times during the night. In the end I just peed out of the window. I hope they never found out.

With Michel and another French friend, together with his American girlfriend Barbara, we travelled in a Citroen 2CV to Dijon where I had my first taste of snails and frogs' legs. Delicious!

Between my Italian and French courses, I had visited the UK to look into possible courses of study starting in the new academic year. My main interest was the teaching of languages, particularly Latin and English as a foreign language. My choice was between an M.Phil at Oxford and an Associateship at the University of London Institute of Education. I chose the latter as it gave me complete freedom to design my course, visit schools and universities throughout Britain, and then produce a report. I was fortunate enough to be offered a British Council scholarship, which not only covered my tuition fees, but also provided me with a monthly stipend and contributed generously to my travel costs.

Visiting schools and university language departments, I was able to gain a good insight into new methods of teaching languages, which I hoped would stand me in good stead on my return to Rhodesia.

One of my visits was to Birmingham University. I was given a lift there by Dr Boaz Shahevitch, a fellow student from Israel. It was snowing in Birmingham and bitterly cold when we set out on the night of 4 March 1965 on our return journey to London. As we were leaving one of the staff warned us about the ice, but Boaz replied, "Don't worry, I've got a wife and two children, so I'm very careful."

Going by car was against my better judgment, since I hate travelling as a passenger with a driver whose ability I don't know, especially in the conditions we were experiencing. Boaz was enormously fat and so was the other passenger, a Miss John from India. She sat in the back and I sat in the front passenger seat. We stopped in Coventry to look at the cathedral, then got back onto the M1. At about 8.25 p.m. (I know the time as the man who later helped us was listening to the radio at the time) the car suddenly hit a patch of ice and slid across the road. The driver tried to correct the skid but failed, and the car swung right around, continuing to skate across the ice in reverse for several hundred yards. It then crashed down a twelve-foot bank at the side of the road, turning over in the process and landing with its bonnet sticking up. When it came to rest we were quite miraculously all alive. I managed to crawl out (through what I don't know). I then opened the driver's door, which was sticking up into the air, and Boaz climbed out. By this time two men had arrived, and after much heaving and exhorting, Miss John was lifted out of the back seat. She was rather shocked, Boaz had a slight scratch across his left cheek, and I had a small cut on the left wrist, caused by my watch strap snapping. (My watch – the one I had bought in Aden – was lost, but this seemed a ludicrously small price to pay for one's life.)

Another motorist, attracted by the beams of light from our car shining into the air, stopped, and we put Miss John into his car. It was freezing outside, with thick snow everywhere. The police were summoned (we had crashed conveniently close to a telephone). An ambulance came as well, as the person reporting the accident spoke of a collision and injuries. About forty-five minutes later, the formalities were completed. The motorist already mentioned took us more than twenty miles to Bedford, from where we caught a train to London. Boaz's car had been extensively damaged.

I had often wondered how I would feel in the face of certain death or serious injury. Strangely, fear was not one of the emotions I experienced. I think it all happened too quickly for that. There was an extraordinary feeling of helplessness, however, as the car just seemed to float across the road. I also felt slightly annoyed at the stupidity of it all. As the car was turning over I was sure that I would hit my head and I had a picture of the mess that this would cause. I also thought of Elizabeth Taylor's spectacular crash in *BUtterfield* 8. Once we came to rest, although

I immediately thought of the possibility of fire, I had no feeling whatsoever of shock or panic. Nor was there any delayed reaction on my part. I was, however, filled with a tremendous amount of gratitude for our escape and for a while was imbued with a strong determination to prove worthy of it, a determination that disappeared after a few weeks.

Being in London was a great experience. I attended the opera, the theatre, the ballet, concerts and films almost every week. Admission for students in the upper circle was very cheap even at Covent Garden. I saw Joan Sutherland in *La Sonambula* and Rudolf Nureyev and Margot Fonteyn in *Romeo and Juliet* (on reflection, I think I saw the latter on my return to London the following year).

During my year at the Institute of Education I stayed in John Adams Hall, one of the University of London's residences. I had a small room containing a narrow single bed, a desk and chair, a washbasin and a two-bar electric heater, which you had to feed with coins. Although the accommodation was rather spartan, the location was perfect – close to the Institute itself, close to lots of public transport, and even within walking distance, if you weren't too lazy, of the West End.

John Adams Hall had a cafeteria, but I often chose to eat out, usually in one of the many Indian restaurants in Drummond Street near Euston Station. Soho, at the time, still had many small food shops and bakeries. So I would often buy excellent cheesecake there, as well as garlic sausage and hot salt beef sandwiches.

I was very fortunate that two of my greatest friends were also in London at the same time as I: Gordon Phillips, who was the archivist at *The Times*, and Willie Marais, who was using his sabbatical to study the piano at the Royal College (or maybe Academy) of Music.

One of my former students from Churchill School, Colin Hoffman, was also in England, having won a Rhodes Scholarship to Oxford. Through him I met a lovely South African girl from

Johannesburg called Gwen Per. Gwen and I became very close. After her return to South Africa we continued to correspond, but eventually the relationship fizzled out. My letters contained big unattributed chunks from the letters Keats wrote to Fanny Brawne. Perhaps Gwen found out!

UDI

Towards the end of my course I had serious doubts about returning to Rhodesia. Under the terms of my scholarship I was expected to do so, but recent political developments there were very disturbing. Garfield Todd had been defeated by Ian Smith, who came to power on a right-wing ticket and threatened to declare Rhodesia's independence from Britain. Officials at the British Council were very supportive and understanding, even suggesting that I might obtain a job with them. However, in the end, missing my friends, I decided to return. Of course, I no longer had a job and my golden handshake meant that I was no longer eligible to rejoin the teaching service on a permanent basis.

Professor Carney offered me a job as a lecturer in the Department of Classics at the University College of Rhodesia and Nyasaland. After a few months, I realised that this was not the right job for me. Although I enjoyed the teaching, I was naturally expected to undertake research on obscure areas of the classics, and this just wasn't me. I missed the cut and thrust of school life. I therefore resigned and was offered a post teaching English at Lord Malvern School in Salisbury. I had hoped that I would be able to teach again at Churchill School, but alas, there was no vacancy.

Lord Malvern was a co-educational comprehensive school; so this was the first time that I had taught girls. I quite liked the more relaxed feel of a mixed school, and it also gave me the opportunity of trying out the Play Way method of teaching English, a method that had so captivated me when I was at Rhodes University. We often spent our lessons outdoors, using role-play, drama, storytelling and other techniques that are mainstream today but were rather revolutionary in Rhodesia at the time.

The headmaster of Lord Malvern School, Ivor John McLachlan, was a bit of a bully. I was personally never affected, but some members of staff and many pupils were victims of his overbearing sarcasm. He ran a very tight ship, insisting on reading every teacher's lesson plans and records every week. Such attention to detail might be regarded as a virtue, except that he spent too much time in the office and too little observing what was really going on. The school had a tannoy system which he most annoyingly abused. If he wanted to see a pupil, he would announce it over the tannoy and every class throughout the school was interrupted. I vowed that no school that I might run in the future would have such a public address system.

Among the teachers at Lord Malvern was Diana Osterberg. She was short, round, jolly and very intelligent, as well as being an excellent teacher. She and I struck up a close friendship.

On Armistice Day, 11 November 1965, after months of abortive negotiations, Prime Minister Ian Smith unilaterally declared Rhodesia's independence from Britain. I was implacably opposed to this decision, not because I was against independence but because of the racial policies that led to UDI and that I knew would be aggravated after it. It was clear to me that my future could not be in Rhodesia. Of course, I did not foresee the long civil war and the subsequent rise of the tyrannical Robert Mugabe. So I can probably count myself as lucky that I decided to leave Rhodesia and return to Europe.

I started applying for teaching jobs in the UK, and was fortunate enough to be offered the post of head of the Latin Department at the High School for Girls in Slough, Buckinghamshire. The appointment was for one term, starting in April 1966, to cover the incumbent teacher's maternity leave.

Meanwhile, because of the imposition by most countries of sanctions against Rhodesia, the government had imposed draconian exchange controls. This meant that almost no money (I think the limit was only a hundred pounds) could be taken out of the country. Actually I did not have any money, since I relied entirely on my teacher's salary. My only asset was my pride and joy, namely my car, a Hillman Minx that I had bought on my return to Rhodesia with my remaining capital. Selling this enabled me to buy my air ticket to London. The money left over was stuck in Rhodesia. However, I had heard of a legal loophole: it was possible to pay for a car in Rhodesia for collection in Europe (not the UK). So I bought a Fiat 850 with the promise that I would be able to collect it from the Fiat factory in Turin when I was ready. I had to take this promise on trust and hope that it would be fulfilled.

This deal left me with almost no cash, and I was now ready to embark on a new life outside Africa. Arriving in the UK, I was literally penniless and could not even pay my rent until I received my first salary. The marvellous headmistress of the school, Miss Gwynneth Owen, had arranged for me to spend the first few weeks with one of the teachers (Mrs Boul) and her husband. They were very kind and hospitable and made me feel very much at home.

Teaching Latin at the High School for Girls was a lot of fun. It was a really well run grammar school, the girls were motivated and the teachers dedicated to helping their pupils succeed. It felt strange at first being the only male on the staff, and it is certainly true that I was rather spoilt by all the attention.

I managed to find digs in Windsor, just a few miles from Slough. My room was in the home of an elderly man named Mr Eastwood. The furniture could be described as charity shop rejects, and in the corner was a very suspect two-ring gas burner and a sink. The communal bathroom was across the hall. It had an ancient, noisy and extremely slow water heater, which took so long to fill the bath that you never needed to open the cold tap, as the first lot of water was cold by the time you got into the bath.

Although I liked Windsor, the distance from the school meant that I had to buy a car. I found an old Standard Eight car, built I think in the late 1940s or early 1950s, for which I paid £70. It did not do much for my image, but it never let me down.

Switzerland

Because my appointment was for only one term, I had to set about seeking another job. Scouring *The Times Educational Supplement* every week I came across an advertisement for the post of Headmaster of the Anglo-American section at the Institut auf dem Rosenberg in St Gallen, Switzerland. It was a long shot but I thought I would apply. To my amazement, I was invited to an interview at the Rubens Hotel near Victoria Station. The interviewer was a Dr Ivor Widlake, the incumbent holder of the post. (I was later told that his doctorate was from a bogus American university from which you could buy degrees.) On Dr Widlake's return to St Gallen, the owner of the school, Dr K Gademann, invited me to fly to Switzerland for a further interview. To my surprise and delight I was offered the job.

As it happened, the Latin teacher whose maternity leave I was covering decided, after giving birth, not to return to the High School for Girls in Slough. Miss Owen, the Headmistress, offered me the permanent position, but by this time I was excited by the prospect of living in Switzerland and running a school (albeit a small one), and so I declined the offer.

I managed to sell my old Standard Eight car for the same price I had paid for it. Now was the time to see if my sanctions-busting arrangement to buy a new Fiat 850 had worked. I contacted the Fiat factory in Turin and was delighted to learn that I could pick up the car there in late July, which I duly did.

Driving this brand new gleaming white car through the busy

streets of Turin and then to Switzerland was quite an ordeal, as it was the first time I had driven on the right. The Italian lakes and the mountain passes were breathtaking in their beauty, and my little car seemed completely at home there.

On the way to St Gallen I stopped off in Geneva, staying the night in the Hotel Bristol on the rue du Mont Blanc, the main road that leads from the railway station to the other side of the lake. I parked my car right outside the hotel. The next day I found a note on the window, with words to this effect: "We know that you are a visitor to Geneva and you are very welcome. But please move your car as this is a no-parking zone." I was really impressed by this friendly attitude. The EE number plates issued by the factory in Turin to show that the car was for export had stood me in good stead.

Then on to the Institut auf dem Rosenberg. The school occupies an attractive site overlooking the town. The facilities were rather rundown, but I was blinded by the excitement of moving to Switzerland and having the chance of running the Anglo-American section of the school. The other sections were German, Swiss and Italian.

The Rosenberg was a boarding school and the Anglo-American section had about sixty pupils aged eleven to eighteen. Most of the international student body took the American College Board tests (SATs and Achievement tests) and some would sit for their GCEs.

Nearly all the staff were new. That should have set off the alarm bells for me, but on the whole they were a professional and idealistic group of teachers. Two long-term teachers bolstered the staff and helped us find our way. They were Marisa Dattilo, who taught Italian, and Betty Guerra, an Indian who taught English. She was one of those dedicated teachers who give their whole lives to the welfare of their pupils. She worked selflessly and unsparingly to help the children at the Rosenberg.

It soon became apparent that education was not really the purpose or priority of the owners of the school. Despite the school's long history, the administration's main interest in the sixties was money. Very few books were provided, facilities were shabby, and teachers were paid a pittance. Indeed, I would say that teachers were the most expendable item and were exploited shamelessly.

Here is an example. One of the pupils was a Prince Michael Mekonnen, nephew of Haile Selassie, then Emperor of Ethiopia. Michael was one of the worst-behaved pupils at the school, arrogant and self-important. One day he disappeared. The blame for this was immediately laid at the feet of his class tutor, who happened to be a teacher in the Anglo-American section. This was despite the fact that he had disappeared from the boys' boarding house with which she had no connection. She was hauled before one of the directors, Mrs Pasch (the dragon-lady who ran the girls' boarding house) and fired. I did my best to intervene on her behalf, but to no avail. The teacher was desperate, as she would be left abroad without an income and with a stain on her record. Fortunately, when I was teaching in Slough I had joined the National Union of Teachers. I contacted the NUT, and even though the teacher concerned was not a member, they undertook to offer her support. They seemed to be aware of the exploitation of foreign teachers in some privately owned Swiss schools. They immediately contacted a St Gallen lawyer who wrote to Dr Gademann, chairman of Rosenberg's board, demanding that the teacher be reinstated. The dismissal was quietly dropped and the teacher completed her year at the school with an unsullied record. (Meanwhile Michael Mekonnnen returned to the school after a couple of days, unharmed and unpunished. He had just gone off to have some fun.)

This incident, plus my frequent confrontations with Dr Gademann and Mrs Pasch over supplies and the treatment of teachers and students, made me realise that one year at the Institut auf dem Rosenberg would be enough. I began to look for another job.

During the Easter vacation I drove to Geneva and visited

the International School of Geneva (widely known by its French abbreviation, Ecolint). Somehow I managed to see the director of the school, Desmond Cole-Baker. Even though Ecolint had no appropriate vacancies, he told me about the Lycée des Nations, a small school on the other side of the lake, that was looking for a new head. He encouraged me to apply, which I did.

The Lycée at the time was going through a crisis. Originally privately owned, it was on the point of closing when it was rescued by a group of parents who formed a cooperative and took over the school. The head left for Paris and the new directors of the cooperative appointed Norma Armstrong, the wife of one of the directors, as an interim head. Her husband was due to be transferred abroad and so they were anxious to find a new head (or Director, as the post was called).

My application for the job was therefore serendipitous. I was invited for an interview by Rolf Liebergesell (who worked for Chrysler) and Lou Mihaly (who worked for Marathon Oil), the chairman and deputy chairman of the Lycée cooperative. Norma Armstrong was also present. Rolf and Lou, both of whom later became friends, were high-powered businessmen and I found the interview quite intimidating. It came as a surprise when, a few days later, I was offered the post. They had contacted all my referees in the UK, Rhodesia and South Africa, all of whom had enthusiastically backed my application.

My salary was to be raised from Sfr 18,000 per annum to Sfr 30,000 (at that time there were eleven Swiss francs to the pound!). What is more, I was invited to bring with me from the Rosenberg any teachers who wanted to come and with whom I was comfortable. Thus Geoff Cox, Adrian Eliott, Arthur Perrow and Peter Keir all resigned from the Rosenberg and joined me at the Lycée des Nations. I had only two regrets at the move from St Gallen: saying goodbye to a great bunch of kids and leaving my beautiful studio apartment in the eaves of a lovely period building.

Finding accommodation in Geneva was not easy. There was

a great shortage of flats at the time. Eventually, I found a small, rather quirky studio in Versoix, a village quite close to the Lycée in Bellevue. The Lycée was housed in a somewhat gothic old house on the rue de Lausanne. It was full of odd passages and rooms of various shapes and sizes. My office was a closed-in verandah.

Within days of the start of my first term as director of the Lycée des Nations, Geoff Cox, who taught chemistry and had come with me from the Institut auf dem Rosenberg, decided to dispose of all the chemicals in the lab. Most of them were unlabelled and undated. He felt he could not trust them. So he placed them all in a bin, which was then duly collected by the Geneva refuse service. Their truck had just gone a few yards down the rue de Lausanne when it started fizzing and steaming. Bangs were also heard. The driver stopped the truck and tipped all the contents onto the road, then came back to the school and quite rightly harangued me for causing what might have been a serious incident. The fire brigade was summoned and they neutralised the chemicals. We had to pay a few hundred francs but were very lucky to have got away with such a paltry cost.

When I arrived, the school took children from kindergarten to grade eight. It was my ambition (shared by the board) to extend the age range to incorporate a full high school. Through Desmond Cole-Baker at Ecolint I had learnt of the International Baccalaureate (IB), a new programme that had only recently started but was already widely accepted by many major universities in the UK, Switzerland, France and a number of other countries. Leading universities in the USA were ready to give advanced placement to students who were successful in the IB. It seemed to me that this was the programme to which we should aspire. Over the next few years, as we added grades, we were accepted as an IB school. I became active in the International Schools Association (which had spawned the International Baccalaureate) and the European Council of International Schools, which was then based in Zurich. We also set up the SGIS, the Swiss Group of

International Schools, and this gave me the opportunity of visiting international schools all over the country. This forward-looking and collaborative approach to education was such a refreshing change from the enclosed and inward-looking attitudes of the Institut auf dem Rosenberg.

Rolf Liebergesell left Geneva during my first year; his successor as chairman, Lou Mihaly, continued to support the changes I was trying to introduce at the Lycée. Sadly, he too was transferred the following year. The new chairman was David Barmes, an Australian who was a senior staff member at the World Health Organization. He was an outstanding chairman, very supportive but at the same time a critical friend, whose ability to keep everyone on the same track was amazing. (David died in 2001 at the age of sixty-nine.)

My right-hand person when I started at the Lycée was the primary school principal, Judith Turner. Judy was a strong-minded, forceful and very energetic educator. She was the person to whom all the staff who were already at the Lycée at the time of my arrival looked to for leadership. Initially, she was suspicious of my intentions for the school and rather resented the fact that several of the teachers had also come from the Rosenberg. But Judy was a real professional and after a few months we worked very well as a team. I trusted and respected her, and interfered very little with her section of the school. After all, I had no experience of that age group and naturally deferred to her greater expertise.

As a staff we went out together most Friday evenings, usually going to a restaurant for '*steack, pommes frites et salade*'. Only later did we discover that 'steack' was generally not beef, but horse!

Among the teachers on the staff was a beautiful young woman named Marjorie Rebeiro who taught the kindergarten. At that time she was going out with Adrian Eliott, a history teacher who had come with me from the Rosenberg. I was very attracted to Marjorie, but both because of my position as her boss and her relationship with Adrian, I made no move. At some point in 1968 she and Adrian split up, and in September Marjorie handed in her notice. She intended to return to India at Christmas as she was under pressure from her family to marry. Her aunt in Bombay was ready to find her a husband.

I tried to persuade Marjorie to withdraw her notice. I invited her to dinner at a restaurant in Coppet, a village between Geneva and Nyon where I was then living. This was ostensibly to discuss her decision to leave, but in the process I made clear my own feelings towards her. She was rather shocked, I think, but not surprised. From then on I courted her, and matters developed rapidly. At the end of October, during the half-term break, we went to London together, and there I bought an engagement ring and asked her to marry me. She was reluctant at first, but eventually 'succumbed'.

On 7 August 1968 I had written the following in my occasional diary: "My only reason for writing again is that I think I have fallen in love. Thirty-two years old, unmarried, I didn't think I would ever find anyone whom I could really love, and yet now I think it has happened: Marjorie Rebeiro, twenty-three, Indian, teacher on our staff, the most delightful person I've known. During the last few days we've spent a lot of time together – mainly in painting the school! I've no idea how she feels about me – somewhat awed, I suspect. Does she return my affections? I don't know; sometimes I feel there is a response, but then too she's not aware of my own feelings towards her. She has such a sweet nature that I am probably mistaking her natural kindness for some kind of love. All I know is that I feel deprived when I am away from her, that I just feel an intense longing to be with her, to see her, hear her voice, maybe just touch her.

"The situation is awkward: she has had something of an affair with Adrian, and I don't know how much they mean to each other. I wouldn't like to hurt either of them. Also my position as director of the school makes our relationship somewhat peculiar. Marjorie still calls me Mr Toubkin. I don't know how things will develop - all I know is that at the moment I love her deeply."

Two days later I wrote the following: "Last night I took the bull by the horns and told Marjorie that I loved her. She was not surprised - it seems she has known it for a long time. God, how I want her. Her own feelings towards me are unsure. Mainly it is fear that seems to haunt her sweet soul: fear of what others will think, her family, friends, above all Adrian and Judy. She seems to feel that Judy will become impossibly jealous, then spiteful and vindictive. Also Marjorie has, until now, enjoyed a good friendship with Judy. Is it worth destroying this?

"Marjorie is incredibly perceptive and sensitive. She seems able to interpret every little gesture, every nuance. Nothing escapes her attention; she is sure Judy is already aware of my growing attachment to her, Marjorie. Yet heaven knows I have never given Judy even the slightest encouragement to believe that I could ever respond to her (Judy). Then there's Adrian, how does he feel to Marjorie? How will he react to my falling in love with her? But it's Marjorie's feelings that are the most important in this matter. Will she love me? Can she love me? Marjorie, my darling, I love you."

If Judy had any feelings for me, I was never aware of them, nor had I ever given her any encouragement. In the event she seemed to take my marriage to Marj in her stride and we continued to have an excellent professional relationship. A couple of years later, after leaving the Lycée des Nations, she returned to her home in Sheffield and married there.

Getting married was never going to be easy. Marjorie was an Indian and a Catholic. I was a secular Jew and a white South African. Marjorie's family (particularly her mother, who was a devout Catholic) were rather shocked but not hostile. My father, who was in any case married to a gentile, was fine about it, but my mother's husband, despite being an atheist himself, was vehemently opposed to our marriage. I have written elsewhere about his opposition, but in brief he threatened to disown me and to prevent my mother and Vicki from having any contact with me if I went ahead with the marriage. This was no idle threat as he carried it out until the end of his life.

Nevertheless, when you are in love, you are not deterred by threats, and Marj and I decided to get married. We agreed to visit Cyprus, where Marjorie's parents lived at the time, so that they would have an opportunity to vet (I mean meet) me. So that Christmas we took a Turkish Airlines flight to Nicosia. It was our intention to spend a couple of weeks there, Marjorie staying with her parents while I stayed nearby in the Dome Hotel. We would take all our meals together in Marjorie's parents' house. We would then return to Geneva and marry there. However, Marjorie's parents seemed to approve of me and suggested that we get married in Nicosia.

Nicosia at the time was a divided city, with the Greeks on one side of the green line and the Turks on the other. My father-in-law-to-be was in Cyprus with the United Nations in the telecommunications department. We knew nobody in Cyprus. So, when our wedding took place on 9 January 1969 in Nicosia's Catholic church, none of the guests was known to us. They were all Bunny's friends and UN colleagues. (Marj's dad, Bernard Rebeiro, was called Bunny by everyone.)

Marjorie looked stunning in her simple white wedding dress, and we looked forward to seeing the wedding photos. But the professional photographer hired for the occasion had omitted to load any film into his camera, so the only photograph we have is a studio portrait taken before the wedding.

Our wedding was on a Thursday. On the following Monday I was due back in Geneva for the start of the new term. So our honeymoon consisted of one night in Kyrenia and one night in Istanbul where we stopped on our return flight to Geneva. Kyrenia is a beautiful and idyllic harbour town, now in the Turkish part of Cyprus. Our only night in Istanbul was a disappointment as we stayed in a grubby hotel and ate in a restaurant whose hygiene standards did not inspire confidence.

On our return to Geneva we lived in my flat in avenue Luserna in Servette, quite close to the city centre. It was a fairly spacious apartment with two bedrooms and two balconies. (Marjorie had been living in a studio flat in Versoix.)

Servette proved to be an excellent location, for in the following year the Lycée des Nations rented a second building in Petit Saconnex, only a few minutes' walk from our flat. This new building, in reality an old house, became the Lycée's high school, allowing the primary school to expand in Bellevue.

Seeking additional space to house an expanded school seemed to become my fate, for it was my constant task both during my five years at the Lycée and my twenty-one years at Southbank International School to look for additional premises. We always seemed to be running out of space.

Not long after our return to Geneva, Dad died. He is buried in a cemetery in East London, South Africa. Marj and I visited his grave during a 'nostalgia' tour of South Africa more than twenty years later.

The first year of our marriage was blessed by the arrival on 30 October 1969 of our beautiful daughter, Nathalie. Marj's labour was very short – Nathalie popped out within a few minutes of the start of labour. She had a shock of dark hair and was absolutely beautiful.

Those early years of marriage and fatherhood were quite difficult. Neither Marj nor I had any experience of real family life. Marj had been at boarding school from the age of seven, while I had been brought up by a single mother before going to boarding school at the age of thirteen. So I think neither of us really knew what to expect of ourselves or of each other. I had a very demanding job with long hours, while Marj felt marooned and lonely in a block of flats without easy access to a garden and without the support of friends and family.

Our bible was Dr Spock's *Baby and Child Care*, which we consulted constantly. Nathalie was generally a good child, although her habit of kneeling in her cot and noisily rocking herself (and her cot) until she fell asleep could be quite unnerving. On one occasion we were driving back from Spain and stopped for a night at a hotel south of Lyon. Once we had assembled Nathalie's cot and put her to bed, she started her rocking motion, which continued for hours. The people in the room above ours began complaining at the disturbance. Eventually, we just packed up and left in the middle of the night to drive the rest of the way to Geneva.

Nathalie's cot accompanied us everywhere. Following Dr Spock, we tried to ensure that Nathalie always had a secure environment which she was used to. The cot was a wooden one from Mothercare and was not easy to assemble, especially by a DIY-phobe like me. So each time we stopped it would take ages to set up the cot. I'm sure Nathalie's teddy bear would have provided sufficient comfort, but we were Dr Spock fundamentalists who tried our best not to stray from his teachings. On one occasion we were driving on a motorway in the UK with the cot strapped onto the car's roof rack. While travelling at probably close to 70 mph in quite windy conditions, the cot blew off. By an enormous stroke of luck there was hardly any traffic on the motorway at the time. Directly behind us was an AA van. The driver immediately stopped and set up some warning triangles and helped us recover the pieces of the cot strewn across the motorway. It was a lucky escape.

Another traveller's tale: in July 1970, when Nathalie was about nine months old, we drove from Geneva to Italy where we spent a lovely couple of weeks in the coastal resort of Alassio. When it came to our return to Geneva we arrived on a rainy evening at the entrance to the Mont Blanc tunnel, ready to drive the short distance from there to Geneva. The Italian immigration official took one look at the cover of my passport and waved us through, shouting "*Inglesi, avanti*". But at the French customs post we were stopped. While my passport and Nathalie's had been issued by the British consulate in Geneva, Marj's passport was an Indian one. Even though it was clear from the stamps in her passport that she was a Swiss resident, the official would not let us pass to drive the few miles across French territory to Geneva. Furthermore, it was the fourteenth of July, Bastille Day, and no other official was available to countermand the refusal or issue a transit visa. So we were forced to drive hundreds of miles further in the middle of the night in pouring rain in order to pass through the St Bernard pass, which connects Italy directly to Switzerland.

Our passports were always a problem. Marj needed a visa for everywhere. So we could not really take advantage of the proximity of France to Geneva as it meant so much advance planning. Today, the Schengen and bilateral agreements make travel between France and Switzerland very easy. My passport, though issued by the British consulate in Geneva and having the appearance of a normal British passport, was in fact a special one with a validity of just six months and issued to Rhodesians abroad. It did not provide any rights of residence in the UK. It was only five years later, after we had moved to Britain and obtained British citizenship, that we were issued with real British passports.

Once, when I was renewing my toxic Rhodesian passport at the British consulate, the consul said that Geneva was a great place to live because of the fifty-two weekends each year when you could get away from it into the mountains. Although I loved the beauty of the mountains, we never seemed prepared for them. During a hot August, Marj and I drove to Zermatt, or at least as close as you can get before cars are banned. Since it was so hot, we wore light summer clothes. Marj in fact wore sandals. But there, on the slopes of the Matterhorn, the mountain did not seem to know it was summer. Marj's feet froze, and she had to borrow socks, shoes and sweaters from an obliging hotel-keeper.

Another run-in with a mountain occurred during a ski trip with a group of students in Italy. I was never able to stay upright on skis for more than two minutes and was a hopeless skier. Nevertheless, on one occasion Marj and I went up the mountain on a T-bar. As we were nearing the top where we were due to dismount we heard someone shout, "Get off!" So we let go the T-bar and duly fell off into the snow, only to find that we were still a long way from the top. The shout had been for someone else who had already arrived. It took us ages to climb to the exit station from which we able to ski, or rather tumble, down the slope.

Once Nathalie was walking, Marj set up a small nursery class in our dining room. This not only provided a useful service, but it also gave Marj more fulfilment.

Nevertheless, the increasing demands of my job, running two campuses about five miles from each other, together with evening board meetings and the constant search for premises and funds, meant that I was often home late. I found it difficult to establish the right work/home life balance. I was beginning to feel that we needed to change our situation.

Though David Barmes was an excellent chairman who provided just the right level of support and constructive criticism, he failed to watch his back and was ousted in a coup by Robert Schmoll. Robert was highly ambitious and had his own ideas about how the school should be run. My laid-back management style and liberal outlook did not suit him. He wanted to run a much tighter ship, eschewing the Lycée's aim of providing a happy and cooperative school community, preferring instead to make the achievement of the highest academic results the primary goal. To me, providing the right sort of environment within the school would lead to high academic standards; to Robert, the standards had to come first. A happy community might or might not ensue; that was irrelevant.

Robert Schmoll assumed almost executive authority,

interfering in much of the day-to-day running of the school. Like a number of other parents in Geneva, he had too much time on his hands. I was frequently undermined by him. I found it very difficult to work with him, though I do not doubt his managerial skills and his enthusiasm. At that time neither he nor I understood the differences in function and responsibilities of a board chairman and the head of the school.

Meanwhile, negotiations were in progress to amalgamate the International School of Geneva (Ecolint), the Lycée des Nations and the United Nations Primary School into a single foundation. Although I did my best on behalf of the Lycée to bring about the new foundation, I was not keen on the idea. Ecolint had run through several director generals. It was run by a vast board whose membership consisted largely of representatives of different international organisations and cantonal representatives. I felt their concern was mainly to protect the interests of their own organisations rather than foster the interests of the school.

The Lycée's cooperative structure, for all its faults, had a small board of individuals who were elected for their skills and views. It was also a requirement of the cooperative that a majority of board members should be Swiss, and it was these members that provided stability and continuity, since the others were more transitory parents. One of our Swiss members, who surprised me by accepting my invitation to join the board, was none other than Jean Piaget, whose theory of cognitive development has had such a profound influence on our understanding of children's learning. (I have to add, though, that he never attended any board meetings.) Other Swiss members, however, were exceptionally helpful, notably Maître Louis Mudry (a leading lawyer), André Bory (property specialist), and Robert Hacco (a businessman who was passionately interested in education). Robert Hacco organised and funded a tour by some of our staff (including me) of some of England's leading progressive schools.

In 1972, we at last succeeded in finding a suitable property for the school. A Catholic boarding school at La Châtaigneraie, about seventeen kilometres from Geneva, was closing. Although a little further from Geneva than we would have liked, its buildings provided an excellent basis on which to develop the Lycée. (On a recent visit to Geneva we took our then four-year-old grandson to a children's football club at the international school in La Châtaigneraie, now a splendid and impressive campus.)

By this time, however, I had decided to leave the Lycée. A number of factors had led me to this decision. On the family side I felt that the long hours required by my work were having a detrimental effect on my marriage, placing an unreasonable strain on Marj and preventing me from spending enough quality time with Nathalie. Professionally, I found it increasingly difficult to work with the new chairman of the board, Robert Schmoll. Our differences in educational philosophy and management style were leading to increasing conflict. Without the family and personal factors I would probably have stayed on and tried to overcome this problem, but the combination of all these pressures led me to resign.

With our passport problems, Marj and I felt that it was important to live somewhere we both felt at home and where our children would become citizens. The United Kingdom seemed the obvious choice.

Britain: our new home

Finding a job in Britain was not easy. I was invited to two interviews, one for the deputy headship of a comprehensive school in Edinburgh, the other for a lectureship in educational technology at the Open University. For the latter post I was entirely unsuitable. The only reason I was invited to the interview was that a friend and former colleague from Churchill School in Rhodesia, David Hawkridge, was the Professor of Educational Technology at the Open University, but I rather let him down at the interview, as my ignorance was totally exposed.

So at the end of July 1972, Marj, Nathalie and I moved to the UK. With our passports we had no right of residence there and were admitted for a temporary stay. Because the pound, already devalued in 1967, had been allowed to float in 1972, our savings in Swiss francs would enable us to live for several months without any income.

Ken Cripwell (alas, now dead), another good friend and former Churchill colleague, was then lecturing at the Institute of Education at London University. He lived with his wife Lorraine and their two daughters, in Park Meadow, Hatfield, Hertfordshire. Park Meadow was a pretty estate consisting of small terrace houses, some with private gardens, all sharing communal landscaped grounds right alongside Hatfield House. He found us a small house to rent on the estate. On arriving there I went to the local comprehensive school and was fortunate enough to be offered a job teaching English. At least we would have a regular income. The only problem was that I needed a work permit. Under the rules in place at that time I had to leave the UK while the school applied for the permit. Madame Kater, an elderly Swiss woman whom Marj had befriended, offered to accommodate me during the wait. So I returned to Geneva, leaving Marj and Nathalie in Hatfield, while I waited for the work permit. Fortunately, it was granted within a couple of weeks and I was able to return to England and start teaching.

Although I enjoyed the teaching, Marj and I had decided that we would look around for a small school that we could run together. Our search took us to various parts of the country. Finally, we found a nursery school in Stroud, Gloucestershire, which we felt was within our budget. Greystones, as it was called, was a substantial Cotswold stone house on a busy road in a rather dowdy market town. The ground floor and first floor had been converted into two large classrooms, while the attic (reached by climbing some very steep steps) consisted of two interlinked rooms with sloping ceilings. This was to be our home, Marj and I using one bedroom, Nathalie the other. We also had the use of a tiny lounge on the first floor and the school kitchen on the ground floor.

A substantial part of our savings was invested as a deposit on Greystones, while the rest of the purchase was financed by Barclays Bank. The manager of the Hatfield branch (in those days bank managers had some authority) had sufficient confidence in us to make a loan.

We arrived in Stroud on a grim winter's evening just after Christmas 1972. We were due to take possession of Greystones the next day. As we lay in bed in a dingy bed and breakfast, Marj and I had a bit of a joint panic attack and seriously considered walking away from the deal. That would have meant losing our ten per cent deposit. However, by morning, we had recovered our self-belief and went ahead with the purchase.

There was no time to lose. Greystones was both a nursery

school and a day nursery, which operated fifty-one weeks of the year (it closed only between Christmas and New Year). So we had to be ready to welcome our first pupils within a couple of days.

Personally I knew very little about nursery education, but I did have some experience of running a school. Marj, of course, had a good knowledge of nursery education. There were five members of staff and space for about forty children for each half-day session. Most of the pupils were children of working mums who would drop them off in the morning and collect them at about 5.00 in the evening. Some were persistently late in collecting their children – that extra half-hour or so at the end of an exhausting day was always frustrating.

Fees at Greystones were very low by today's standards, even taking inflation into account. They were due to be paid weekly, mostly in cash. So at the end of each week, Marj and I would sit in the kitchen counting piles of coins. I felt a bit like Silas Marner.

When we arrived we found that the staff were paid appallingly little. Sarah, the youngest member, received only £4 a week. We immediately raised salaries significantly. Of course that meant that we would have to raise fees, which we did a few months later. I have never felt that it was right for staff to subsidise tuition fees by taking home low wages.

Nathalie was not very happy at Greystones. She found it difficult being in one of the nursery classes while her mum and dad were somewhere else in the building. Eventually we found her a place in another nursery school on a half-day basis where she could interact with other children her age without the presence of her parents.

On 22 June 1973, our son André was born in the maternity wing of Stroud hospital. Labour was again quite short, though he took longer to arrive than Nathalie. When Nathalie was born in Geneva, she was immediately washed by the nurses and wrapped in swaddling clothes before being handed to Marj. In Stroud,

André was immediately placed at Marj's breast. He was covered in blood and still attached to the umbilical cord and placenta. I nearly fainted at the sight and felt quite ill. I much preferred the Swiss experience.

While Marj ran the nursery my main tasks were preparing lunches for forty children and looking after the administration, including the payroll. Needing a challenge, I enrolled at Bristol University, which was about thirty miles from Stroud. I drove there three times a week, having prepared the lunches in advance. I had chosen to do a diploma in educational administration. It turned out to be a poor choice as it was very dry and related mainly to local authority administration. Although I stuck with the course and attended lectures and tutorials, I decided not to write the essays or dissertation as I did not want to spend so much time researching a subject in which I had little interest.

Although Stroud is a rather drab town, it is located in the midst of some glorious countryside and is surrounded by lovely Cotswold villages, which we used to enjoy visiting at weekends.

Our work at Greystones was pretty intense. Marj in particular was extremely busy, sometimes not stepping outside the nursery for days on end. Despite the busy lives we led, I felt professionally very unfulfilled. I also missed Geneva and wanted to return there even though I knew that I had no job. So in July 1974 we appointed one of the staff as manager of Greystones, packed up once again and moved back to Geneva.

Thanks to the help of André Bory, a Swiss member of the board of the Lycée des Nations, we found a flat in Meyrin, a newish suburb close to Geneva airport. Our move was very risky, as we had no source of income except for a trickle from Greystones. Still, I have always taken an optimistic view of employment prospects. Knowing that there was no suitable educational leadership job available in Geneva, I explored other possibilities, and was interviewed for jobs in hotel management and banking. I had written a personal letter to the head of the

Swiss Banking Corporation in Zurich. It seems he passed on the letter to the Geneva manager of SBS who invited me for an interview in the mistaken belief that his boss wanted him to see me! He soon discovered that I knew nothing about banking when he asked me what I thought about gilts. I waffled some reply and he did not offer me a job.

I applied to the education department in Geneva for a teaching job, and was surprised to be offered a position teaching English as a foreign language at the Ecole de commerce André-Chavanne, a state secondary school. It was very well equipped, classes were small and the students on the whole well motivated. I had about fifteen class hours a week, and it was probably the easiest teaching job I had ever had. Although quite well paid, I had to supplement my income by teaching a couple of nights a week at the University of Geneva. There, I taught English as a foreign language, but the circumstances were totally different. The class was enormous, probably in excess of a hundred students. This reminded me of the Italian class I had attended in Perugia. It was totally unsuited to the teaching of a foreign language.

This period in our life was a very happy one from a family point of view. My work was less demanding and I was able to spend more time with Marj and the children. We enrolled Nathalie in the United Nations School. (Fortunately their kindergarten fees were lower than their regular school fees.)

Our stay in Geneva was cut short by problems at Greystones Nursery School in Stroud. We felt we had no choice but to pack up and return to the UK. We drove to Le Touquet in our aging Fiat estate car. Instead of crossing the channel by ferry we loaded the car onto an old cargo plane, strapped ourselves into the crude seats, and flew to Lydd in Kent.

This time we rented a lovely bungalow in Bisley, a charming Cotswold village about ten miles from Stroud. The rear of the house faced onto open fields while the front led to the village. Nathalie attended the local school where she was very happy.

André, a rather adventurous child, went wandering on one occasion out of the garden and onto the road (admittedly a very quiet one).

Greystones once again became the centre of our lives, but at least we were no longer living 'above the shop'. We subsequently bought a tiny former council house very close to Greystones. It cost £7500, which was still a lot more than we could really afford.

Meanwhile, I started applying for jobs. One of these was the post of Principal of the Hyde Park branch of the American Community School in London. Invited for an interview by Gordon Speed, the co-owner of ACS, I was impressed by the quality of the facilities located in two lovely Georgian houses in South Kensington. After my interview I put on my coat and discovered after I got back to my hotel that it wasn't mine. I had taken a much higher quality coat that must have belonged to Gordon Speed! Of course, I phoned the school and returned it at once. I thought my faux pas might influence the outcome of the interview, but was pleased to be offered the job.

My appointment as Principal at ACS was due to start at the beginning of August 1976. One of the teachers allowed me to use her flat in Hampstead while she spent the summer vacation in the USA. Finding accommodation for my family was my top priority, but this was no easy task at the time. Privately rented flats and houses were quite rare then, and by the start of the school year in September I still had not succeeded in finding accommodation. Instead, each week, I lived in different bed and breakfasts from Mondays to Fridays, then rushed back to Stroud for the weekend. It was not a satisfactory arrangement.

Eventually, I managed to find suitable accommodation in Wimbledon. We rented the two upper floors of a late Victorian house (the ground floor was rented to someone else). It was located in a quiet street, though rather close to the railway line, and was within walking distance of the American Community School's Wimbledon branch. The children of ACS staff were able to attend their schools free of charge if they met their admissions standards. So Nathalie was admitted to ACS Wimbledon where she received an excellent education. Marj would walk her there every day, pushing André in the stroller. Meanwhile I would travel by underground to ACS Hyde Park in South Kensington.

A few months later, after selling our little house in Stroud, we bought a three-bedroomed semi-detached corner house quite close to our rented property in Wimbledon. Although rather neglected, it was delightfully situated in a quiet street and overlooked Dundonald recreation ground. It cost £19,500, an amount that stretched our meagre resources to the limit.

For the next two years I ran ACS Hyde Park. It was an elementary and middle school, catering for children aged five to thirteen. I was lucky to have as my assistant principal Kim Betts, an excellent administrator who ensured that everything ran smoothly. Working alongside Gordon Speed, the co-owner of ACS, was not easy, but he seemed to be satisfied with my work as he offered me the post of principal of ACS's high school in Knightsbridge from the start of the 1978/9 academic year. With the opening of yet another ACS branch in Cobham, Surrey, the previous principal of ACS Knightsbridge was appointed as superintendent of all the ACS branches. He was John Paterson, whom I had first met when we acted together when I was a student at Rhodes University and whom I met again when I was director of the Lycée des Nations International School in Geneva and he was headmaster of the Commonwealth-American School in Lausanne.

Running a high school was much more in my area of expertise. ACS Knightsbridge was housed in two extravagantly refurbished adjacent buildings in Pont Street and Lennox Gardens. One of the buildings had previously been the Danish embassy and the local corner shop was Harrods. I had a very grand office with a magnificent fireplace, leather-topped desk and two leather chesterfield sofas. Outside my door was a uniformed

Me, aged about ten, in
Gonubie Mouth

Mom with her parents and siblings

Me at about thirty

In Paris 1964

Marj and I on our wedding day

Dad, not long before he died

Nathalie and André

Mom with Nathalie
and André

The four of us

With Nathalie
and André

Marj and André

Marj and I at a Southbank Prom

With André on his high school graduation

André graduating from
SOAS

Southbank Kensington

Glenda Jackson opens Soutbank Hampstead. Jane Treftz (right)

1986 me 50,
André 13

Emilie at Southbank
alumni event

With Mom and Stella

The whole family in Cape Town

With my sister Vicki

With my sisters Barbi (L) and Gail (R)

Mom and I

Four generations

Marj with her
sister Lourdes

Nathalie at eighteen

André and Nathalie on their wedding day

Me at 75 with Luce, Marj and Nathalie

Presented to Marj for organising garden party

André and Nathalie with Emilie, Léo and Emma

Emma and Léo

Nigel, Ben Jane, me

commissionaire who also controlled entry to the elaborately furnished and chandeliered reception area. My office was designed to impress and intimidate, isolated from the rest of the school and completely unsuited to my temperament and management style. Getting around the school, with its myriad narrow corridors and staircases, was difficult. There was no central space where students could gather, nor was there any outside space. Students not in class sat against the walls of St Columba's church opposite the school.

The school had many fine teachers as well as a generally motivated student body. The curriculum was a fairly standard American high school programme. College Board exams (SATs and Achievement Tests) were taken and a number of students also took a few Advanced Placement tests, the traditional route to good American universities.

Although the school was doing well, I became increasingly disillusioned with the owners of the school. Their obsession with cleanliness and tidiness was very oppressive in a building without 'breathing' space for its students. Furthermore, their treatment of staff was arbitrary and often unjust, and salaries were exploitative. Unlike the primary and middle school teachers at ACS Hyde Park, the high school teachers at ACS Knightsbridge did not take injustices lying down. They made their feelings known and I supported their complaints. This often led to disagreements with Gordon Speed and Manny Poularis, the owners of ACS. At the end of the year Gordon Speed wanted me out of Knightsbridge. Since sacking me would have been difficult, he wanted to transfer me to ACS Wimbledon, another elementary and middle school. Obviously this would have been convenient for me as we had bought a house there, but I regarded this transfer as constructive dismissal and decided to resign from ACS. This was a rather risky thing to do as I had no prospect of another job, but I felt I could no longer work for ACS. I therefore gave notice of my intention to leave at the end of the school year. Gordon Speed told me I could "rot in hell" and that I was on his "shit list"!

Ensconced in my grand office, I reflected on what I was doing there. Yes, I had all the trappings of power – a leather-topped desk and all that and 'protected' by a uniformed commissionaire. The trappings of power, yes, but isolated from the real work of the school that went on beyond the chandeliers. My main task as principal seemed to be to ensure that this grand building should be kept in a pristine state. The only interest of the school's owners seemed to be building maintenance. Education came rather low down on their list of priorities.

As I reflected on this sorry state of affairs, the head of English, David Tucker, came into my office. In the course of a wide-ranging discussion, David suggested that we should start our own school. As it happened, I had been thinking along the same lines myself. I had recently read *The School without Walls* by John Bremer and Michael von Moschzisker. It told the story of the Parkway Program in Philadelphia, a programme set up in response to the abysmal public education system in that city. Instead of a purely classroom-based curriculum, the programme drew on the resources of the city – its museums, galleries, businesses and other enterprises. I was really excited by this idea, believing that London had even more to offer. Indeed, I doubt whether there is another city in the world that can offer as much as London.

After reading the book, David was equally excited, so much so that he was unable to keep quiet about it and shared the idea with some of his colleagues, who immediately expressed their interest in joining us.

David Tucker was head of English at ACS Knightsbridge. With a master's degree from the University of Wisconsin and a PhD from University College London, he was an expert on Charles Dickens. Married to an English actress at the National Theatre, David was an exciting teacher who seemed well suited to undertake the kind of project we had in mind.

John Marberry was David's closest colleague in the English department. He was a brilliant, demanding, charismatic teacher who did not suffer fools gladly. Bright students adored him and would do anything for him. Some of the weaker students and those of less conscientious habits found him intimidating.

His wife, Susan, was a teacher in the Social Studies department. Very bright and hard-working, she was a fine teacher who could bring history to life. Both she and John were very interested in all the arts, soaking up London's theatre, music and art scene.

The fifth member of our group was Stephen Bailey, who taught chemistry. Steve was a graduate of MIT, probably one of the most gifted and intelligent people I have ever known. He could turn his hand to anything. Not only was he an inspiring teacher, but he was also a fine sportsman. He had an easy, relaxed manner that appealed to students. He was an excellent organiser and a great problem-solver. He was one of those people who could immediately grasp the kernel of any problem and discard all extraneous matter. A very valuable person to have on board.

A Leap in the Dark

On 12 September 1979, the five of us crowded into the cramped Dickensian office of Nutt & Oliver, a firm of City solicitors, to sign a document which established the American International School (as Southbank was then called).

Of course, signing a piece of paper is not the same thing as getting a school up and running. Up to that point all we had was the idea. Although I had given up my job as principal of the American Community School, my four colleagues continued teaching for another year.

Throughout the spring and summer we used to meet, usually in a café at the National Theatre, to discuss the kind of school we wanted to establish. Deciding a name proved one of the most difficult issues. We all agreed that the words 'International School' had to be included. We ran through a long list of possibilities, including Churchill and several American presidents (Jefferson, Franklin, Washington, Kennedy), as well as the United Nations. We would have liked the name London International School, but that was too close to the International School of London, which already existed. In the end we settled on the American International School or AIS. Because four of the five founders were American and we all thought that most of our students would be bound for American universities, the word American seemed quite natural.

Three principles guided our planning for the new school: it would be democratic, it would use London as the classroom, and the curriculum would be individual. (We later added a fourth principle: the school would be international.)

When we founded Southbank in 1979, the writings of three educators had the strongest influence on my thinking. The first, as already mentioned, was John Bremer, whose book *A School without Walls* described the Philadelphia Parkway Program. This inspired the idea of using London as the classroom, an idea Southbank still tries to pursue but which we took much more literally in the early days when Southbank was only a high school.

The second influence was John Holt, whose writings inspire me still. Books such as *Why Children Fail* and *Why Children Learn* reveal greater insight into the development of a child than any other writings I have ever come across.

The third strong influence on me was the writing of that extraordinary Japanese educator, Shinichi Suzuki, famous above all for his revolutionary methods of teaching young children to play the violin. This concept we later incorporated into the curriculum when we opened our primary school.

Our decision to start a school with no money, no financial backing and no building would by most standards seem at best audacious and at worst rather stupid. But I remembered a story told by Suzuki in his autobiographical book *Nurtured with Love*:

'*Life was wretched in Japan right after the end of World War II. The winters in Matsumoto are severe, and there are days when the temperature falls to 13 or 18 degrees below zero centigrade. On one of those days my sister returned from an errand, and as she shook off the snow she said, "In all this cold, there is a wounded soldier standing on the bridge down by the Hon-Machi, begging. He is standing there shivering in this driving snow, and nobody is putting any money in the box at his feet... I wanted to invite him in to sit in our kotatsu in our warm room and give him some tea." I immediately replied, "You merely wanted to?" She said, "Yes," and suddenly ran into the street. I* made the room warmer, stirred up the fire in the kotatsu, got out some cookies somebody had sent us as a gift, and waited. About thirty minutes later my sister came back with the white-clad wounded soldier... Koji and I urged him into the kotatsu with us, and we sat and talked about all sorts of things.

Afterwards my sister said to me, "You taught me an excellent lesson." Indeed it was our first lesson in "If you want to do something, do it."... There is no merit in just thinking about doing something. The result is exactly the same as not thinking about it. It is only doing the thing that counts... The habit of action – this, I think, is the most important thing we must acquire.'

My decision to leave ACS without securing another job first obviously had serious personal consequences. We no longer had an income, we had to give up the Ford Cortina that ACS had provided, and – most serious of all – we had to withdraw Nathalie from ACS Wimbledon, as we could not afford the tuition fees. Instead, she transferred to Wimbledon Chase Middle School close to our house. (The Local Authority had at first placed her in another school much further away, but we managed to persuade them to change their minds.) Wimbledon Chase was quite a good school, though it was not able to offer the quality of education provided by ACS.

I liked the headmaster, Ian Hardy, and thought highly of him until 1982, when the school was used in the making of the film *P'tang Yang Kipperbang*. The producers of the film did not want any non-white children to appear in the film. One of the excluded children, a girl of mixed race, complained that it was not fair that she was excluded but that Nathalie (whose mother was Indian) was not. So, despite the fact that Nathalie was probably lighter skinned than many of her fellow pupils, Mr Hardy excluded her from appearing in the film. I was appalled, not only for Nathalie but for any other children whose racial background may have prevented them from taking part in the film. This, of course, was before legislation against racial discrimination had been introduced. My disgust with race discrimination had been the main reason why I left Rhodesia and South Africa, and here it was being applied in my daughter's school in London. I am sure Ian Hardy was not racist, but he displayed a sad lack of leadership on this occasion.

André attended Dundonald Primary School, which was just across the park from our house. It was a singularly uninspiring school. The most vivid image I have of the school is the sight of the headmaster's caravan parked in the school driveway on the last day of each term. As soon as the children were dismissed, he drove off in his caravan and was not seen again until the first day of the new term.

With no job, two young children and a mortgage, our financial position was pretty dire. I was asked to tutor a couple of my former pupils from ACS and this provided a trickle of income. One of them lived on the edge of Richmond Park. Sometimes, at the end of the lesson, the family chauffeur would drive me home in their Rolls Royce, a rather incongruous sight in Rayleigh Road!

To get some money, Marj gave up the gold bangles she had received, in the Indian tradition, on her marriage. I took them to Hatton Garden, the centre of the jewellery trade in London. Though they were all 24-carat gold, the bangles were not hallmarked. However, I managed to sell them for about £1000, enough to keep us going for a couple of months. We were lucky that the price of gold had rocketed during the summer of 1979.

Rob Kuehn, the husband of Janet Kuehn who was head of the social studies department at ACS, was the principal of Richmond College, an American-style university. He offered me a part-time post as a lecturer in English as a foreign language. This was very helpful, as it gave us a small but steady income, and also allowed me to spend the afternoons looking for premises for our new school venture. I used to cycle from our house to the college, a distance of about nine miles each way. Much of the route was across Richmond Park, a really enjoyable ride. It was at Richmond College that I met Avi Chandiok, an accountancy lecturer, who later became the auditor of our school's accounts and a good friend.

By Christmas 1979, we had still not found any premises for the school. I felt I had to devote myself full-time to the search. We had negotiated an overdraft of £20,000 with my bank (Barclays Bank, Hatfield, which had helped Marj and me to finance our earlier purchase of Greystones Nursery School). My fellow directors, all of whom were still teaching full-time at ACS, agreed that I should be paid £500 a month to enable me to give up my job at Richmond College to look for a building and get started on developing our project.

Looking for premises was a depressing job, as we were turned away by one estate agent after another, sometimes sympathetically but usually with a sneer – until, that is, we met Douglas Blausten of Cyril Leonard & Co. Douglas did not laugh at us. He seemed to grasp the concept of the school and found us an old Victorian primary school in Cornwall Road, close to Waterloo Station and the National Theatre. It had been a Catholic primary school run by the Franciscans. It consisted of four large classrooms on two floors, plus two small rooms and a tiny kitchen. Attached was a hall/gym and a tarmac playground. The hall was not part of our demise but we were permitted to use it. The Church retained a small chapel above the hall.

We immediately set about renovating the building. Having no money, we had to do it all ourselves. Everyone joined in, including our spouses and children and some of our future students who intended to transfer from ACS to AIS. Every spare hour was spent in sanding, scraping and painting. I have always hated DIY. For this project there was no choice, but working together as a team was wonderful.

Thanks to a government scheme for small-scale entrepreneurs, I was enrolled on a course at the City University. It was run by an organisation called Urbed. The state scheme covered not only the fees but also a small stipend (I think it was £40 per week), which at that time was extremely helpful. We used to meet once a week and I found the course invaluable. Ronnie Lessem, now a professor at the University of Buckingham, was an excellent teacher. The most important lesson I learned was 'never run out of money'. This stood us in good stead when we were struggling to survive. Profits are of course important, but cash flow is absolutely essential.

Southbank International School - a school without walls

London of course already had several 'international' schools, but all of them seemed either American or British in orientation. Marymount was certainly an international school, but it was an all-girls school and was run by a religious order. So we intended to be the first truly international school in London. This was to be achieved not simply by recruiting international students and teachers, but by promoting an international outlook and developing an international curriculum.

Although the American International School was set up as a limited company, we intended it to be as democratic as possible and to run it as a cooperative. It was our intention to make all staff shareholders and to include all students in making decisions that affected them.

I can't say the idea of failure never crossed my mind. I can't say that at all - it did quite often. What also crossed my mind was that if you didn't have a go, you would always regret it. As always, 'It's better to have loved and lost than never to have loved at all.'

Thanks to the efforts of a PR friend of David Tucker's, the school received some wonderful early publicity. I had lunch in May 1980 with Peter Wilby, then editor of *The Times Educational Supplement*. He was intrigued by the concept of the school and wrote a favourable article in the *TES*. Later in the summer articles appeared in a number of national newspapers, including a very encouraging one in the *Sunday Telegraph* magazine. To crown it all, on the day the school opened in September 1980, a film crew from the BBC followed our students around London. This was shown on an early evening programme called *Nationwide*. All this publicity, while not producing many students directly, nevertheless gave the school a certain credibility and status well beyond its deserts at the time.

We felt that London itself was an incomparable resource. At the time the educational programmes of most galleries and museums were very underdeveloped. By basing ourselves in central London, we had easy access to them. But it wasn't simply museums and galleries that were available. The whole of the South Bank complex was within a few minutes' walk of our little building in Waterloo. The National Theatre in particular proved a very valuable space, because its acres of lobbies and corridors were clean, comfortable and, above all, empty. So we often conducted classes and seminars there without anyone ever questioning our presence. I used to teach my own English class in the empty public spaces of the National Theatre. Without labs, we arranged to use the well-equipped labs of what is now South Bank University. Where we couldn't offer a course, for example in music or certain languages, we arranged for students to take these at institutions like Morley College or the City Lit. We also drew on experts and professionals to teach courses or classes in their own specialities.

Some examples: History lessons held in the British Museum (the teacher, Anton Powell, was a lecturer there); Dickens taught on the very streets that he wrote about (the teacher, David Tucker, now runs London Walks); Science taught in the labs of what is now South Bank University; Drama taught by a director from the National Theatre.

With only two indoor toilets (the outside toilets had been converted into a music room), even that essential function required a journey: to the pub across the road if you were desperate or to the National Theatre if you weren't!

So using London has always been a basic tenet of the school. We could also have adopted as our motto, 'Necessity is the mother of invention'.

All of this helped to create a particularly dynamic and exciting programme. Many students responded with enthusiasm at being treated as young adults, responsible to a large degree for their own learning. Others found the freedom too tempting. Most teachers also enjoyed the challenge and the opportunity of trying something different.

This sort of programme is a white-knuckle ride. It's exhilarating, but those with weak stomachs find it too scary. It demands a lot of confidence and a lot of trust on the part of the faculty and parents. Those who always like to be in control would find it too difficult. It involves risk, but then all human advances do.

Gradually, as the school grew, as pressure increased for measurable results, as the practical difficulty of keeping so many balls in the air simultaneously exceeded our juggling skills, more order was introduced. It's a fact of history that pioneers and explorers eventually settle down, and that's what we did.

But the idea of a school without walls is not confined to the physical environment. Indeed, I would say that the most important walls to escape from are those that surround our minds. Those are the walls that prevent us from seeing, and more importantly experiencing, what goes on outside.

So I believe that a school without walls is really a state of mind. Even when Southbank became a more settled, stable place, the most important thing that we tried to preserve – I hope with some success – was an openness to the outside world, a readiness to see other points of view, and an acceptance of people who might be different from ourselves. A school without walls means that we know that we don't know everything, we are constantly in search of knowledge, we are not afraid of something new or different, we are willing to risk failure. It means not always going for the easy option.

Imbued with more idealism than common sense, Southbank started out as a highly democratic body. We ran the school as a cooperative, with all full-time members of staff holding equal shares.

However, it did not stop there. We introduced the Town Meeting, a forum for all members of the school: students, teachers, support staff, even parents if they happened to come along. We discussed and decided almost everything by majority vote on a show of hands. Often, debates would become so heated and intense that classes would be suspended in order to complete the Town Meeting. Was smoking allowed? Was it OK to go to the pub over the road? Was attendance at classes compulsory? What sanctions were acceptable?

I considered the debate to be part of the education. Something I do strongly believe is that education is very much a process and not simply a product. That doesn't mean there isn't a product at the end, but the process is more important. So debating issues is important. A lot of what passes for education is just learning a chunk of knowledge that is not particularly meaningful. Whether you learn one chunk of knowledge rather than another does not make you an educated person. But thinking clearly and solving problems, meeting your goals, creating something worthwhile, developing understanding and appreciation – these things make an educated person. Although there are many different ways of achieving these attributes, facing a problem and trying to resolve it (which was what we were often doing at those Town Meetings) contributed significantly to the educational process. I think that the students who went through it, and perhaps the adults as well, will have learned something important. But it probably wasn't the best way of marketing a school.

When the school inspectors (HMIs – Her Majesty's Inspectors) visited the school, they were intrigued by the Town Meeting that took place during their visit. I think that strongly influenced their decision to grant us permission to continue the school despite our primitive facilities. The HMIs were not box-tickers, but genuine educators.

It was at one such Town Meeting that the name of Southbank was adopted. The name was proposed by Nigel Hughes, then a maths teacher but subsequently my successor as the school's head. At the time the international school world was awash with acronyms: ASL, ISL, ACS, TASIS, ICS. (Come to think of it, it still is.) To add to the confusion, we were AIS. The change of name to Southbank was probably one of the few proposals adopted unanimously by a Town Meeting. And, despite our peregrinations north of the river, it has stuck.

The later Town Meetings seem so tame in comparison, but what a relief! Why did the school not continue to operate in the same democratic manner? A serious difference of opinion on educational philosophy between two staff factions, each with its own following of students and parents, tore the school apart and nearly led to its demise at the end of its first year. We realised that power without responsibility was dangerous. Slowly and painfully, the school emerged from that dark chapter in its life. We realised that there had to be structures in place that reflected the different levels of responsibility that we held. In particular, it was clear that the board was responsible for the school's financial well-being and for approving policies.

But despite this change of structure, Southbank remained, by school standards, a pretty democratic place. Most decisions were taken after widespread consultation and every effort was made to achieve consensus. The school remained open to new ideas and listened to the views of all.

The night before the school opened in September 1980, there was still no timetable. Instead, pinned on a wall was a long list of our eighty or so students and beside each name were the names of the courses each student was interested in taking. The faculty all stood around this list and bargained about who would be teaching or supervising what and when! Somehow, because each of us took personal responsibility, it worked.

At first the owners of ACS (the American Community School) did their best to shut us down. A private detective posing as the parent of a potential student questioned me closely about my views on ACS. As he left he revealed that he had recorded our conversation, but fortunately I had not said anything too derogatory, not because I suspected him but because I felt it would be unprofessional to have done so.

ACS claimed the name The American International School was theirs, and they threatened to take legal action against us. Of course, they had never used that name, though apparently they had registered it as soon as we opened. We had not been aware of the need to register our name. After a while I realised that they were just trying to distract us from our main task and get us ensnared in legal proceedings, which would have bankrupted us. So we decided simply to ignore their threats, a tactic which seemed to work, for we heard no more. Over the years that followed, our relations with ACS became cordial and cooperative.

For all of us, that first year was probably one of the most exciting of our lives. It was a high-wire act, but each of us was willing to catch anyone who tripped. What started so optimistically that year ended in bitterness and recrimination. It led to the forced resignation of one of the founders, John Marberry. The staff, students and parents were bitterly divided over the issue. Our democratic structure meant that there were endless meetings and confrontations.

The way we handled John Marberry's departure was appalling. I would have dealt with it much more professionally in my later years; there should have been much earlier intervention. We allowed matters to develop to such an explosive point that there was no longer room or time for discussion.

I do not know if the end result would have been different. We might still have agreed to a parting of the ways, but it might have been an amicable parting as opposed to a bitter one. I think we inflicted unnecessary hurt on John and his wife, Susan, and nearly destroyed the school in the process. And as headmaster at the time, I have to accept the responsibility.

When we started the school there was some discussion as to whether there should even be a head of the school. Eventually, I was voted unopposed as headmaster. The idea was that there would be an annual election. John Marberry's departure definitely undermined my position. The staff discussed whether I was the right person to be head of the school, but they decided there was nobody else – so I was elected by default. No further elections were held and it never became an issue after that. In the manner of Idi Amin, I seemed to become Headmaster for Life, or at least until my retirement in 2001!

At the end of our second year the school was in financial difficulties. During the course of that year we took two pay cuts, the first of ten per cent, the second of fifteen per cent. All of us took these pay cuts, an illustration perhaps of the advantage of running as a cooperative. At the end of the year we had managed to negotiate a slightly larger overdraft but not much. I think we increased it from £20,000 to £30,000. David Tucker, Steve Bailey, our registrar Lesley Milton and I put up our homes as collateral. We had got behind in payments to certain institutions, in particular the South Bank Polytechnic – we had to pay for the use of their labs. I had to go round to renegotiate payments, all of which we honoured; it just took us longer.

We were seriously thinking of closing, of being forced to close because we just didn't have enough funds. I think this was another occasion when the cooperative structure worked, in that all of us saw we had to do something. We all had a lot to lose. So together we agreed to tighten our belts and carry on. And from then on I can really say that the direction of the school was always up. There were good years and not-so-good years but the school has never again been in financial trouble. In spite of a subsequent fraudulent use of the school's funds, we generally managed to balance our accounts. We never saved much but we never got ourselves into debt and always managed to pay our way.

In our second year we had a mathematics teacher, John Nyman, who was a professor from Hunter College (City University of New York) on sabbatical for a year. He suggested, when we were making all these salary cuts, that we really needed to employ people on an hourly basis. We had too many staff who were part of the fixed costs. We needed more flexibility. That's when we started the idea of cooperating tutors and employed more people in that capacity.

Things have changed a bit since then and the school's core group has grown again with a higher proportion on fixed salaries. But this is somewhat dangerous because you don't have much flexibility. If you look at the fixed costs of the school there are just two things that matter – the salaries and the rent. The rent is fixed by contract and if you add that to the salaries you are probably talking about 80% of the school's budget. The rest is peanuts. There is now a third major cost and that is Information Technology. If you buy a few less books or a few more books or a few less staples it doesn't make a difference at all – they are minor costs in the overall budget.

So when John Nyman proposed this particular way of employing part-time staff, we decided to do so. Actually, it's the way that most tutorial colleges and language schools work. The trouble with it is the level of commitment that can be expected from staff. I don't mean Southbank's cooperating tutors were not committed – they were – and many worked extremely hard at the school, way beyond the call of duty. But on the whole people who have other commitments elsewhere can obviously give only a certain amount of time to the school because they have other lives as well, whereas a full-time staff member, when needed, can really be called upon – and usually willingly. It was not ideal but it was a way of keeping afloat and gaining some control over staff expenditure. If necessary we could reduce our use of cooperating tutors by increasing the amount of time full-time staff worked. I don't think we ever really had to do so, but the possibility was there. Ironically, part-time staff now legally have all the rights of full-time employees!

When enrolment started picking up in our third year it was clear that we had outgrown Cornwall Road. We had outgrown it partly because our programme had changed. It was becoming a little more conventional. This was largely in response to what parents were demanding even though they knew what kind of school Southbank was. They were anxious for their children to be passing exams, though nobody could have complained about our college placements. We had wonderful college placements in those first few years, including three at Princeton: Fuad and Irfan Kamal and Bill Glockner. We had no college counsellor, but each teacher worked hard to ensure that his or her advisees were placed in universities of their choice. And, of course, we had many exceptional students!

The Great Trek North

One of the recurring themes at Southbank (and it's still recurring!) was shortage of space. Our little old schoolhouse on the South Bank was bursting at the seams when, in 1982, we managed to lease a lovely Georgian building a few minutes' walk from Victoria Station. Our great trek north had begun.

Once again it was thanks to Douglas Blausten that we found this building. It was located in Eccleston Square and belonged to Davies's School of English, part of the worldwide Eurocentres language group. They had three adjoining buildings in Ecceleston Square, but were using only two of them. So this third building was available to rent.

In comparison with our previous location, we were definitely moving upmarket. Unlike the building at Waterloo, the new one had no outside space, except for a tempting but inaccessible garden belonging to the square. Not that we needed the garden for exercise. The new building was six tall storeys high. Climbing up and down those steps all day kept us at the peak of physical fitness. Once again we made use of outside facilities, including the Queen Mother Sports Centre and a sports hall near the Elephant and Castle.

Architecture undoubtedly influences behaviour. Southbank's move from Cornwall Road, Waterloo, to a beautiful Georgian house in Eccleston Square, on the Belgravia/Pimlico border, changed the behaviour of both students and staff. Waterloo, then surrounded by decaying industrial warehouses and social housing and in the middle of a growing arts scene, was an 'anything goes' area, ideal for the school's early days. It seemed to encourage what some might deem as bizarre or chaotic behaviour. Eccleston Square on the other hand was rather posh (at least comparatively) and demanded more conventional behaviour.

Of course, signing up for the International Baccalaureate immediately changed the way the school worked. The fact that Lesley Milton and I (the registrar and headmaster respectively) had our own offices and the faculty had a dedicated staff room, however crowded, also changed things. In Cornwall Road, even though full-time staff had a desk somewhere in the building, there was no private space. Students and teachers were constantly mixing, but now in Eccleston Square there was a definite separation. It made life more comfortable and perhaps more efficient, but that easy communication and the feeling that we were all equal partners in a shared enterprise were definitely lost. At Cornwall Road, if a student couldn't find a place to work, he or she would just commandeer the desk of one of the teachers. I remember one day finding Irfan Kamal sitting at my desk with a sign 'coup d'état' prominently displayed. At Eccleston Square, that would have been unthinkable.

The basement of the building was shared with Davies's School of English next door. This gave us access to a hall and a professionally run cafeteria, which served real food (i.e. if you liked soggy chips). For the first time we had a library and a staff room and an office with a door. In Waterloo some of the teachers had shared a windowless coal cellar. Now we had a room with windows and a sink. It seemed like real luxury.

After one year there we expanded downwards slightly to incorporate a middle school. That's when Jane Treftz, later principal of Southbank Hampstead, joined us. I had known Jane for many years when she was a teacher and then assistant principal at the American Community School's Wimbledon campus. She had a great reputation as both teacher and administrator, and

I was delighted when she joined Southbank. She took over as the teacher of middle school, grades seven and eight, which we then called Junior High. (It was only when we moved to Notting Hill that a real middle school could be developed.) I felt it was important to recognise the very different needs of eleven- to thirteen-year-olds. In Jane, we had the ideal person to achieve this.

The following year we introduced the International Baccalaureate. Since I had introduced the IB to the school I headed in Geneva for several years, I was familiar with it. Its introduction was not opposed by the staff. In fact, there was more opposition to the later dropping of the GCSE and the adoption of the IB's Middle Years Programme (MYP) than there was to the IB Diploma at the time. I think people were beginning to feel the need to have something solid. We were still doing the odd GCSE, the odd A level and American SATs and APs, but our population was beginning to change. We had a lot of Scandinavians at that time, particularly Norwegians, who didn't really have an interest in O or A levels or GCSEs or SATs – they were interested in a qualification acceptable at home. It also seemed a good idea to affirm our internationalness. Robert Blackburn, the Director General of the IB, came and talked to the staff and parents; as a result everyone was very positive about it.

I would say we never looked back after that. I think we had about nine students in our first year when the IB began. I remember Hortencia Calder successfully teaching a group of IB students Spanish (not *ab initio*, but the full Language B) from scratch. Most of the students obtained the IB Diploma. I think the highest score was 32. We were very proud of that – we thought it was a great achievement at the time, though that score is now lower than Southbank's long-term average. In addition to the IB, we were running a high school diploma programme, which somehow we tried to link together.

The arrival of Anne Lawday (aka Adler) changed the face of Southbank's drama programme. Until then it had consisted of the occasional play directed by a volunteer member of staff. But Anne introduced a more professional approach. Southbank became one of the pilot schools in the IB's Theatre Arts programme. She not only directed many memorable plays but also, by producing several musicals of high quality (even though the school had virtually no music programme at the time), succeeded in getting almost the entire school involved in drama.

It did not take long before we ran out of space again and rented a small annexe around the corner in St George's Drive, more or less diagonally opposite Eccleston Square. It consisted of three floors of a rather less attractive building shared with other users. It was not an entirely satisfactory solution but it enabled us to cope for a while.

By 1988, Southbank had completely outgrown its building in Eccleston Square and its annexe in St George's Drive. In any case, our lease had come to an end and the owners of the main building wanted their premises back for expansion of their language school next door. The search for a new property had begun.

Finally, we found a building in Harrington Gardens, South Kensington, with the necessary planning permission. It was occupied at the time by Lansdowne College. Negotiations were completed and by the end of June 1988 the staff had packed up everything and we were ready to leave. Then came the blow. We had been gazumped! This was at the height of the property boom, and gazumping (i.e. outbidding someone after a price had been agreed) was rife. Boston University, whose pockets were much deeper than ours, had made an offer that the owners of Harrington Gardens could not refuse.

Fortunately, our landlords in Eccleston Square very kindly agreed to our staying on for a while longer while our search continued. And that's when 36/38 Kensington Park Road in Notting Hill came into the picture. It was empty at the time, having been acquired by a property developer. Its most recent use had been that of a bail hostel (i.e. a hostel for people awaiting trial). Although it did not have full planning consent as a school, its particular planning category allowed it to be used as a boarding school. We thought that would be sufficient to allow us to move in. I was fortunately still naive enough to believe that if it had combined educational and residential use, what difference would it make? We would simply use more of it for education and less for living.

That was not, however, the view of the neighbours and local authorities. Only after a tortuous and nail-biting struggle was planning permission granted. The local authorities were absolutely adamant: they were going to put an order on the premises to shut us down, and they wouldn't allow us to start. The neighbours were up in arms. We had a very articulate neighbour – Nick Ross, a well-known BBC presenter – who expressed the strong opposition of the locals to the establishment of a school in Kensington Park Road.

At the public meeting which we called, we were able to deal with many of the questions people had. But we were obliged to give hostages to fortune, such us limiting the total number of weeks that we could use the building each year because we claimed that one of the advantages of a school was that for several months of the year it was largely unused. Another was that we would not allow ball games or music in the garden, which was to become the playground.

Some would say that throughout my career I seem to have been willing to take risks involving some rather 'grey areas'. How do I justify this? I would say sometimes necessity makes one act in a certain way. I would much rather we were fully legal, but I do not think we have ever broken the criminal law. I would put it on a par with double parking or occasionally exceeding the speed limit without driving dangerously.

The school owes an enormous debt to our solicitor, Stephen Wegg-Prosser, a Southbank parent at the time. His skill and tireless devotion helped us gain acceptance. Long after his son

Ben had left Southbank, Stephen continued to help the school in every possible way.

As a bail hostel, the building had been divided into minute bedrooms. It took a great leap of imagination and faith to believe that somehow it could be converted into a school. One of the parents, Francis Oeser, an Australian architect (and accomplished poet), kindly offered to redesign the building and oversee the conversion work. He is another one of Southbank's unsung heroes, putting in endless hours of his time to ensure that the building was fit for a school.

In December 1988 we packed up once again. The move was scheduled to take place during the Christmas holidays, with school due to start in the first week of January. But the building was far from ready. It was covered with scaffolding and there was mud everywhere, but we decided to move in regardless. The cooperation we received from everyone was fantastic. Stepping over buckets and mops, paint pots and ladders, we managed to start school just four days after the scheduled starting date. Building materials were scattered about, no noisy work could take place while classes were in session. It was certainly not easy, but the good humour of both students and staff (and of the Yugoslav construction team too) got us through the painful start. I must pay special tribute to Ed Sterling. As always, Ed just took upon himself the responsibility of ensuring that the move took place with as little disruption as possible. He must have worked day and night throughout the 'vacation'. And special mention should be made of Patricia Frischer, who organised every aspect of the move.

Thus was Southbank Kensington born

Notting Hill was an area that was new to us. That is one of the reasons we chose to move in the middle of a school year, figuring that parents would not withdraw their children at that time. Our hope was that by the end of the school year everyone would be used to the area and the new commute and would not pull out. The strategy worked. Notting Hill was not then the upmarket area that it is today. Though it was beginning to improve, the public perception was still of a rather rough and seedy part of London. I remember a letter from an irate parent (a famous actress who lived in Belgravia) complaining that her daughter now had to travel to such an insalubrious area. Today, of course, Notting Hill is one of the most desirable parts of London. It is a matter of great regret that the school was not able to purchase the freehold of the property at the time. The subsequent increase in the value of the property would have helped to solve many of Southbank's later building problems.

Although we had more room than at Eccleston Square, we soon outgrew the facility. Next door to the school was a car rental company, which used the ground floor and basement garage of a block of flats. One day I noticed that the company had disappeared. So I asked Harold Rantor, a parent and property consultant who was looking for additional space for us, to investigate. It turned out that the owners of the freehold were interested in letting it to us. The property consisted of a showroom fronting Kensington Park Road and two floors of garages at the rear (Portobello Road).

The garages were dark, dingy and covered in grease. It required some vision to see their potential. When it was completed, it provided us with greatly improved facilities, which included a home for the Janet Kuehn library, an art room, another science lab, a computer lab, a music room and a hall. Until then, we had been obliged to rent hall space from the Kensington Temple across the street and St John's Church a couple of blocks away.

The new building was opened by Nick Ross, our next-door neighbour who had so vociferously opposed the school's initial occupation of 36/38 Kensington Park Road. His participation in the ceremony was an indication that Southbank was now an accepted part of the local community.

I had always been keen to open a primary school as a feeder for the middle and high school, though I thought it would be in a separate building. However, we decided to open it in part of the 'new' building, as the new acquisition was known. To do so took some persuasion. Not everybody believed that it was the right thing to do. I thought then, and even more so now, that it was the right decision. It was an area of the school where enrolment was very strong and I think it added a huge amount to the school's quality of life. Jane Treftz, who had done such a great job in making our middle school a success, was the obvious choice as the first principal of Southbank's primary and middle school.

In opening the primary school we were trying to develop a coherent philosophy that matched our philosophy for the rest of the school. We wanted the new primary section to retain the same ethos. Indeed the primary school would allow us to develop the open-minded values in our students from a young age in the hope and expectation that these would continue throughout their time at Southbank. (The IB Primary Years Programme had not yet been established.)

I had long been inspired by the ideas of Shinichi Suzuki, and it seemed natural that we should give every child the opportunity of learning to play the violin through the Suzuki method. We were fortunate in obtaining the services of Alison Apley, one of London's leading Suzuki violin teachers, to run the programme. Though some initially grumbled about the demands of the programme and questioned the value of requiring every child to learn the violin, the Suzuki programme has been one of the great successes of the school at both Kensington and later Hampstead, where Alison continued the excellent work she had started at Kensington. Hampstead expanded the programme with the addition of Suzuki cello tuition.

One of the things we thought would match Southbank's philosophy well was the teaching of a foreign language from the early years. This seemed to be natural for an IB international school. It was also decided that the foreign language taught in the primary school would be German. The choice of German raised some eyebrows, but there were several reasons for it. French was already established as the first foreign language in the middle school and Spanish in the high school. At the time of glasnost, the reunification of Germany, the collapse of the Iron Curtain and the opening up of Eastern Europe, the choice of German made sense. It was and still is the home language spoken by more people in Europe than any other.

German and Suzuki would show that we were different. Not just to be different – the choice obviously had to match our educational thinking – but I think both of those areas succeeded in making the school stand out.

Information Technology was also a feature of the primary curriculum. While that is commonplace today, at the time it was quite unusual.

A small anecdote: the Kensington campus has several precious parking spaces at the rear of the building in Portobello Road. One day, Jane Treftz and I needed to use the school's minibus, which was parked parallel to the back wall and very close to it. Someone's car was parked at right angles behind it. Try as I might, I could not manoeuvre the minibus onto the road. So Jane and I left the minibus and went to look for the owner of the obstructing car. When we got back, lo and behold we found the minibus neatly parked on Portobello Road. I had left the handbrake off and the minibus had gently rolled onto the road on its own without hitting either the obstructing car or any passing traffic.

A new name and new campuses

In the closing years of the millennium, the school changed its name again, this time to Southbank International School. When Nigel Hughes had proposed to a Town Meeting in 1980 that the name of the school be changed to Southbank, it became known as Southbank – The American International School or Southbank AIS. Once the school adopted the International Baccalaureate as its main curriculum, the make-up of the student body became more diverse. The school's brief flirtation with GCSEs increased the proportion of British students. The word 'American' in the school's name became increasingly inappropriate. Yet many felt that we might lose students if the word 'American' were dropped. Besides, it was part of the school's history.

But in the mid-90s the school abandoned the GCSE and switched totally to an IB curriculum, with the intention of adopting the IB Primary Years and Middle Years programmes as well. The school's contorted attempts to please everybody simultaneously were no longer tenable. Southbank clearly was and intended to remain an international school. The time had come to rename the school Southbank International School. Any fear that this would adversely affect the school's intake of American students proved unfounded. In fact, since the word 'American,' was dropped from its name, the number and proportion of American students increased significantly!

The departure of Lesley Milton left a huge gap in the school's administration. I had known Mary Langford when she was the School Secretary at the Hampstead International School (ironically, housed at 16 Netherhall Gardens, which became the future home of Southbank's Hampstead campus). When she joined Southbank as Assistant to the Headmaster I was delighted, for Mary was far more than a secretary. She was an internationally minded educator, a networker par excellence, a problem solver and a doer. Though initially she rubbed some people up the wrong way, Mary proved invaluable to the school over the years. When we set up a separate admissions department to cope with the opening of the Hampstead campus she proved the ideal candidate to undertake the daunting task of ensuring that our enrolment grew sufficiently fast to sustain both campuses.

Mary transformed Southbank's admissions process, which until her arrival had always been rather haphazard. With her networking skills she ensured that Southbank's strengths became more widely known. She interpreted her role of admissions director as far more than mere admissions. She actively supported the PTAs at both campuses, always took a lead in such events as International Day and Open Day. In fact Mary had a finger in almost every pie. She could always make things happen.

Mary also made us more conscious of our students (and their parents) as global nomads. She ran several highly effective workshops for staff on this theme, as well as arranging for outside specialists in this field, such as Barbara Schaetti, to spend time at the school.

For years, music had been Southbank's Cinderella, but when we obtained the hall in Kensington Park Road and opened the primary school, it was time for Cinderella to come to the ball. She arrived in a blaze of energy and dynamism in the form of Dan Laubacher, who single-handedly made music matter. A gifted musician, composer and teacher, Dan established a choir, a school orchestra, taught music to all classes (primary and middle school), supported the Suzuki violin programme, introduced music as an IB subject, composed and directed a musical, and established the Southbank International Youth Orchestra which provided Southbank students with the opportunity of playing with young professional musicians. Sadly, the SIYO did not survive Dan's departure, but he laid the foundations for Southbank's flourishing music programme.

Back in the early eighties the school had acquired its first computer. There was great excitement as Steve Bailey demonstrated the marvels of its 48K capacity. Personally, I couldn't see what all the fuss was about. Nor was I convinced of the value of computers, even after Nigel Hughes and I attended a workshop in Manchester (lovely hotel, by the way) to learn about the BBC Acorn computer for schools. It took a whole weekend to learn how to programme a straight line – I thought a ruler and pencil were far more effective.

How times have changed! Could we live without computers today? Two people really put computers on the map at Southbank. Firstly, Marcia Wallin, who set up our IT programme, designed the first computer lab, wrote the database programme that served the school for many years, taught students, staff and many parents to use the computers, and managed to extract what at the time seemed like a blank cheque from the board to invest in equipment.

Next came Eric Perlberg, a man of extraordinary intelligence and drive. He saw technology as a tool to be used throughout the curriculum and in every area of school life. With the backing of Southbank's board he established ASW2 (A School without Walls 2), an exciting online school. Many Southbank students benefited from this programme.

The pioneering work done by Marcia and Eric was consolidated and extended by Russell Webley and a team of IT teachers on every campus. Today computing plays an integral part in the education of every student at every level at Southbank International School.

Such was the demand for places in the primary school that

we were soon, once again, in search of additional premises near the Kensington campus. A couple of years earlier, 16 Netherhall Gardens in Hampstead had been offered to us, but we had turned it down as it was not in our area. The building had previously housed a branch of the American Community School. It was then sold to the owner of North Bridge House School, also in Netherhall Gardens. He decided to continue it as the Hampstead International School, until the building was condemned as unsafe. The building itself belonged to a Catholic Church organisation. They redeveloped the site, but were obliged by the local authority to rebuild the school with an identical facade and to ensure that it was used only for educational purposes. They were therefore looking for an educational institution to lease it.

The Hampstead location didn't quite fit into our planning although it did fit into a strategy that I had several times advocated at our board meetings, a strategy of having more than one primary school and middle school feeding into a single high school. Parents will let their older children move around but they prefer to have their younger children reasonably close to home. I had seen this work extremely well at ACS where their primary/middle schools in Hampstead, Wimbledon and South Kensington fed into their high school in Knightsbridge. So in that sense Hampstead fitted into a long-term strategy.

Thus Southbank obtained a brand-new purpose-built school with the elegant appearance of an Edwardian house. Jane Treftz, who had been the first principal of Southbank Kensington's primary and middle school, became the principal of Southbank Hampstead, which opened in September 1995. Had we appointed an outsider, I am not saying it would not have been successful, but it would not have had a Southbank ethos. It probably would have gone off in a different direction, especially with my rather non-prescriptive management style. It was a tough decision for Jane, but a crucial one for the school. At Kensington, she had begun to develop a successful primary and middle school and had around her a well-tested structure. Now she would be alone. Of course, the management and administration of the school would continue to support her. I divided my time unequally between the two campuses and a few teachers taught in both campuses. Ben Joseph put in an enormous amount of time to provide the facilities and organise the building work required to adapt the premises to our purposes.

Jane provided the leadership that made Hampstead an outstanding international primary and middle school. The report of the Independent Schools Inspectorate confirmed this. In fact, the report on Southbank Hampstead was the most favourable I had ever read.

The official opening of Southbank Hampstead was performed by the local Member of Parliament, Glenda Jackson, winner of two Oscars. *The Times* wondered why a Labour MP would open an independent school, but Glenda Jackson, in a letter to the editor, wrote an excellent riposte, ending with these words: "The future peace and prosperity of the world depend on good international relations. Given the appalling mess the Prime Minister (John Major) is making of our relationship with the European Union, perhaps he might like to spend a couple of terms at Southbank school."

Although the new building opened a new catchment area for Southbank, it did little to relieve the pressure on Kensington. So the search continued. We found another building in Notting Hill Gate. Potentially it could have been a great building. It had a huge warehouse, which could have been converted into a gym. The premises were large enough without serious modifications to hold and expand our primary school and would have created space in Kensington Park Road.

It was owned by London Electricity, who supported our planning application. Unfortunately, our application for planning permission was turned down by the local council. And who was the chair of the planning committee? None other than one of the local councillors who had always opposed our presence in Kensington Park Road. Even though he recused himself from the planning meeting, I have no doubt he was delighted with the decision. In summary, the Council informed us that it was not in the interests of the Royal Borough to authorise a change of use for a school that would predominantly serve the children of foreign expatriate business professionals!

After years of searching, a beautiful listed building in Portland Place was found in 2002. (This was after my retirement, but I was still a member of the Board at the time.) Because of its listed status the building had to be carefully adapted to use as a school. Every aspect of the building work required the approval of English Heritage. At last, in September 2003, Southbank Westminster opened its doors. The high school and Kensington's middle school moved into the new premises. Meanwhile Kensington was remodelled as a primary school (Early Childhood to grade five). This meant a major change in the character of the Southbank Kensington school, as one of its attractions had been the family feel created by the community of three- to eighteen-year-olds. However, both buildings provided exceptional facilities for all their students.

One of the most appealing features of the IB programme is CAS: Creativity, Action, Service. It is, however, a difficult area to implement effectively. Because it formed an important part of the overall development of students, Southbank always gave it a high profile. But the arrival of Phyl Clancy lifted the programme to an entirely different level. She forged links with voluntary groups throughout London. Under her leadership, students volunteered to help the elderly, young children, the disadvantaged and the disabled. Students became imbued with a sense of service and many realised that helping others was both humbling and rewarding. Southbank must have one of the best urban community service programmes anywhere.

In later years and until recently, Southbank supported the

Mwereni School in Moshe, Tanzania, a school that also caters for blind children. Students, teachers and parents from Southbank regularly spent time at Mwereni, helping with both teaching and building projects. They raised many thousands of pounds to support the school. A local street has now been named Southbank International School Road in recognition of the part played by Southbank.

Southbank Hampstead had linked up with the Jack Taylor School, a state school for severely disabled children aged five to nineteen, in its first year thanks to Shari Sapp, a Southbank parent with twins, one of whom was in the Early Childhood class at Hampstead, the other at the Jack Taylor School. In 1999, Southbank Hampstead's principal, Jane Treftz, applied to the Department of Education for funding a partnership between two school communities with differences. She had a vision of opening minds and broadening experiences of students and teachers by bringing two very different schools together. In 2000, Southbank Hampstead received a grant of around £22,000. This enabled the schools to embark on a number of joint projects, including drama and music sessions; technology, numeracy and literacy projects; fundraising events, school trips, sports day; assemblies; staff meetings; etc.

The effects of the partnership were profound. Children overcame the fear of their differences, and when Southbank enrolled a disabled girl, the mother reported that, whereas she was teased about her disability in previous mainstream schools, at Southbank this had not even been mentioned once by any of her classmates. One Southbank parent said: "I think this relationship is invaluable for what it teaches our children - compassion, understanding, tolerance and respect for all people; that underneath we are all basically the same." The success of the partnership secured ongoing funding over the years.

The idea of action and service are central not only to the IB Diploma programme but also to the Middle Years Programme

(MYP) and Primary Years Programme (PYP). Thus in every grade, students were involved in community service. This was a crucial part of the Southbank ethos.

The school always took an active part in organisations promoting international education. One of the first steps, taken during the school's first year, was to apply for membership of the European Council of International Schools (ECIS). Members of Southbank's faculty became team members for ECIS accreditation visits to schools in many parts of the world.

Southbank was one of the founding members of the London International Schools Association in 1981 and remained an active member afterwards.

To strengthen its ties with British schools, Southbank became a member of the Independent Schools Association. This was also the route the school chose in seeking accreditation under the auspices of the Independent Schools Joint Council, a federation of all the leading independent schools' organisations throughout England. The head and principals were active members of accreditation teams to other schools.

When Southbank decided to adopt the International Baccalaureate Diploma, it became actively involved in the workshops and teacher education programmes run by the IBO.

This participation was hugely expanded as a result of the adoption of the IB Primary Years Programme (PYP) and the IB Middle Years Programme (MYP).

Many of the staff became examiners not only for the IB but also the GCSE. Some also became valued presenters for the IB.

The establishment of IBSCA (The IB Schools and Colleges Association) in the UK was also actively supported by Southbank International School. Nigel Hughes chaired this organisation for several years.

From its beginning, the make-up of Southbank's student body was international. The changes in the nationality profile of the students were often a barometer of world political and economic events.

In the school's first year (1980/1), the largest group was Iranian. This coincided with the Iranian revolution. Most of Southbank's Iranian students were hoping to proceed to American universities after graduation. Their numbers dwindled as it became increasingly difficult to transfer funds from Iran to the UK. The number of Lebanese students increased during the terrible conflict in that country.

When Brit Warren joined the staff in 1981 she set about recruiting students for what we then called the Scandinavian Studies Department. Although the numbers varied, there was always a significant number of Scandinavians at Southbank. At one time the Swedes were the largest group in the school, but economic changes led many Swedes to return to Sweden. Norwegians and then Finns took their place. Whatever the composition, the Nordic countries remained a significant section of Southbank's population.

An increase in the number of Japanese students in the late eighties and early nineties led to their being the dominant non-English speaking group in the school. Again, however, the downturn in the Japanese economy led to the return of many families to Japan. Glasnost, Perestroika and the collapse of the Berlin wall created a sudden surge of students from Russia and other East European states. Later, many Israelis joined the school. There was always a solid core of British and American students. The British population declined somewhat after the school dropped the GCSE exams in the mid-nineties. When I retired, there were more than sixty nationalities represented in the student body.

One of Southbank's unique features was its language programme. From the very beginning it was possible for a student to study virtually any language. While the school offered French, Spanish and German (at different age levels) as core subjects, many students opted to study their own language or another foreign language. In any one year as many as twenty languages were being studied. These included most modern European languages, as well as Japanese, Arabic, Hebrew, Mandarin and Swahili. Although economics forced the school to charge for these additional languages, it resulted in a rich and diverse programme taught by an amazing range of teachers, mainly part-time, who enriched the school with their own culture and experience. It also meant that the learning of other languages was seen as something quite normal.

Southbank people

In the beginning, advisors (i.e. class teachers) provided the college counselling for their students. Subsequently, Nigel Hughes and Anne Lawday (Adler) combined the job of college counsellor with their heavy teaching loads. But in the mid-nineties we felt that the growth of the school required the appointment of someone who could devote more time to the task. We were extremely fortunate in obtaining the services of Gwen Martinez, who had wide international experience. She was a British graduate who also held a degree in counselling from Harvard. An outstanding organiser, Gwen transformed the counselling department. She was a leading light in the counselling field and became chair of the ECIS group of counsellors. During her time at Southbank, Gwen went on to obtain both a Master's degree and a doctorate from Boston University. Later she took on the role of IB Coordinator, a job that neatly complemented that of Director of Guidance.

A little earlier we had recognised the need for students to have a personal counsellor. This role had previously been undertaken by the advisors, but as the school grew not all advisors felt comfortable in this role. Students, too, wanted and needed more expert and confidential help. Vaughan Emmerson, a brilliant English teacher, undertook further studies in counselling and was appointed to this role. After he took a break from Southbank, Katherine Fox, another fine English teacher who also studied counselling, became the school's personal counsellor.

The faculty, too, represented many different countries. With some twenty languages taught at the school, teachers were drawn from countries where those languages were spoken. But in addition, Southbank sought teachers, whatever their national origins, who had experience of teaching in countries other than their own. This rich mix was always one of the school's major strengths.

The school had reason to be proud of the achievements of its faculty beyond the confines of Southbank itself. To mention just a few:

Ray Monk, who taught the Theory of Knowledge, became a bestselling and award-winning biographer. His books on Wittgenstein and Bertrand Russell have received wide acclaim. He is now Professor of Philosophy at the University of Southampton.

Eivor Martinus, who taught Swedish at Southbank, is well known for her stage and TV adaptations of Strindberg's plays in English, for which she too has received awards.

Elisabeth Norr, who taught German in Southbank's first year, went on to found one of Norway's leading international schools, Skagerak International School, in Sandefjord. I was privileged to be the guest speaker at her school's first graduation ceremony.

Several faculty members became principals of other international schools, among them David Harrold in Turkey and Mary Langford in Spain and London.

In the arts, Dan Laubacher, while continuing to inspire students as a teacher, has become a successful composer, and Patricia Frischer, founder of Southbank's art programme and now based in San Diego, is widely acclaimed for her paintings. Amy Bartow Melia, the first director of the London International Gallery of Children's Art (LIGCA), headed a major education department in the National Museum of American History at the Smithsonian in Washington.

In the context of international schools, Southbank had a good record of retaining staff. When I retired in 2001 I had been at Southbank for twenty-two years. This length of service was exceeded by several others, including Nigel Hughes (my successor as Southbank's head), Ben Joseph (former biology teacher who became the school's finance director) and Hortencia Calder (an excellent Spanish teacher).

It is always invidious to single out individual students. There are so many who have gone on to make significant contributions to their communities. I have lost touch with many of them and hope we can re-establish contact. Facebook has certainly helped in this regard.

A few stick in my memory for reasons that are not always clear. Among them was Eliene Ferreira from Brazil. Eliene was from a large, impoverished family, but she had been adopted by a wealthy Brazilian couple who came to London as the husband was the Brazilian Minister here. Eliene was thirteen years old and virtually illiterate, having had almost no schooling. Jane Treftz and I interviewed her and her adoptive mother. Other schools had turned her down, but she had such a sparkling personality and an expressed determination to make the most of her opportunities that Jane and I decided to admit her even though we knew we would be heavily criticised for doing so. We need not have worried. Within months, Eliene was speaking English fluently and was one of those students whose sunny and positive outlook on life raised everyone's spirits. She had a real literary flair. A poem she wrote about her two mothers moved me to tears. Eliene left Southbank at the age of sixteen when the family was transferred to Montevideo. She obtained an IB Diploma, but sadly I have heard that Eliene was killed in a road accident. In her short life she brought joy to so many.

Then there was Mirna Jancic, whose family had fled Bosnia-Herzegovina during the civil war in the former Yugoslavia. Her father had been a diplomat and a published poet and playwright, but they had arrived in the UK with virtually nothing. Despite their considerably reduced circumstances,

Mirna was determined to succeed and went on to achieve an excellent IB Diploma.

I remember Taorid Ogbaru, a student from Nigeria in the school's earliest days. A childhood illness had left Taorid with one leg shorter than the other, but he was immensely strong. One day four of us were struggling to move a safe from the ground floor into the basement. We just could not budge it. Taorid saw us, crouched and then lifted the safe onto his back and carried it down the stairs. I don't think this word was in use at the time, but we were 'gobsmacked'! Taorid also proved to be a man of his word. When he left Southbank his fees had not yet been paid, apparently because of problems transferring money from Nigeria. He assured us that the money would be paid, but frankly we were convinced that the amount would simply have to be written off. Many months later, however, Taorid turned up and paid his bill in full.

With good reason, Southbank had a policy of not admitting students who did not live with a parent or guardian. With Michael Hunter, a student from Dalhart, Texas (a tiny town in the Texas panhandle) we made an exception, and what an excellent decision that proved to be. Not only was Michael an outstanding student who contributed to every aspect of school life, but he turned out to be a playwright of some distinction. As part of his IB Theatre Arts project he wrote, directed and acted in a play called *The Box*. After the IB he went to Edinburgh University where he continued to shine and direct productions at the Edinburgh Fringe Festival. Some years ago Marj and I were in Edinburgh for the annual festival and we had the privilege of attending another play directed by Michael. I understand that he is now an adjunct professor at Stanford University.

One of my abiding memories was of a Japanese student (whose name I have forgotten) during the school's first year. Although he was a gifted mathematician nobody knew anything else about him, as he never said a word to anyone. Even though the students were friendly, his continued reticence meant that after a while nobody sought his company. After six months in the school he suddenly stood up at a Town Meeting and carefully and slowly read from a piece of paper: "My father is being transferred back to Japan. Before I leave this school I want to talk English. Please help me." He received a tremendous ovation, and from that moment on was never alone. By the time he left a few months later he was speaking pretty good English.

When he joined Southbank in 1983 at the age of ten, Benjamin Wegg-Prosser was by far the youngest student in the school (we had only a high school at that time). But he was also the most precocious. He even stood for the presidency of the Student Council at the age of eleven! (He was not elected.) Benjamin was one of those students who would volunteer for everything. Despite his amazingly busy life he was always ready to try something new. It was largely due to his voraciously devoured general knowledge that Southbank won the inter-school quiz bowl the year he was on the team. He had a passion for politics, which he subsequently studied at Sheffield University. During his vacations he worked for Jack Straw (later Foreign Secretary) at the House of Commons. On graduating from university he became the personal adviser to Peter Mandelson, a prominent member of the new Labour government in 1997, quitting only after Mandelson's first fall from grace. He subsequently became Tony Blair's Director of Strategic Communications and is now a high-powered consultant.

Anthony Stern was, with his equally memorable brother Paul, one of the first British students at Southbank. He was in my advisory group and he was my only Latin student at the time. Needless to say he went on to get a good IB Diploma and studied at Durham University before entering Sandhurst, the British military academy. When Southbank celebrated its twenty-first anniversary in 2001, Anthony, by then Major Stern, was invited to be the guest speaker at the school's high school graduation. It was a particularly proud moment for all of us who knew

Anthony. Colonel Tony Stern is now Military Attaché at the British embassy in Myanmar.

The annual Graduation Day, at which Southbank students graduate from high school, is probably the most prestigious day of the year. In the early days the venue varied. The first ceremony was held in the Wigmore Hall. Subsequent venues included the Royal Court Theatre, the National Film Theatre, the Royal Overseas League (a regular venue until Southbank outgrew its facilities) and the Kensington Temple. From the mid-nineties, however, the school has held the graduation in Church House next to Westminster Abbey. The wonderful circular hall, which was temporarily used to house Parliament after the Houses of Parliament were bombed during the Second World War, provides a wonderful setting for the graduation, helping to make it a memorable occasion for everyone. The graduation was held on a Saturday morning and was followed by a Prom in the evening.

Although students were dressed in caps and gowns, the graduation ceremony was always celebratory rather than formal. This was helped by many of the brilliant guest speakers the school had over the years. Some that spring to mind are Magnus Pyke (scientist and broadcaster), Baroness Seear (Leader of the Liberal Party in the House of Lords), Sam Wannamaker (the actor who inspired the rebuilding of Shakespeare's Globe Theatre in London's Bankside) and Jeff Thompson (scientist, professor at the University of Bath, and international educator par excellence).

At the 2000 graduation the guest speaker was George Walker, Director-General of the International Baccalaureate Organization. During his speech he announced that Southbank had been approved as a centre for the IB Middle Years Programme, thus making Southbank the first school in the UK to be approved for all three IB programmes – Primary Years, Middle Years and the IB Diploma.

Some of the speakers were more home-grown, parents of Southbank students, but no less distinguished. These included

Pier Salinger (President John F Kennedy's press spokesman), Alberto Aza (the Spanish ambassador), Miklos Nemeth (former Prime Minister of Hungary and the man who opened the borders to allow East Germans to flee to the West), and David Bodanis (scientist and award-winning author). One whose speech touched the hearts of all who heard her was Thyra Heaven (wife of the Jamaican High Commissioner and distinguished in her own right). At the fifteenth graduation ceremony the speaker was one of the school's founders, Stephen Bailey, who had been a much-loved teacher at Southbank. And for the twenty-first anniversary, Major Anthony Stern, a student from the school's earliest years and whom I have mentioned before, inspired us all.

Two years after my retirement, I found myself in the unusual position of giving, not the headmaster's address, but the guest speaker's. I felt very privileged to be in such distinguished company. I was invited again as guest speaker in 2009.

Over the years, Southbank welcomed many distinguished visitors. Among them was Tom the Masai warrior, who thrilled all of us with his stories of life in the Kenyan bush. Liv Ullman, the famous Swedish actress, spoke to us about the work of UNESCO for which she was an ambassador. But undoubtedly the most exciting visitor was Superman himself, none other than Christopher Reeve. I remember how it came about. He was appearing in *The Aspern Papers* on the West End stage, together with Vanessa Redgrave and Wendy Hiller. Jane Treftz suggested to Billy Kuehn, a keen drama student, that he write to Christopher Reeve and invite him to the school. To our amazement, he accepted. His visit was kept a secret. All the students and staff gathered in the hall at Eccleston Square for what they thought was a routine Town Meeting. When Christopher Reeve walked into the hall the place erupted. As later events showed (i.e. after his paralysing accident), he was a man of great passion, courage and intelligence, and even during his address to Southbank those qualities were evident.

When I was head of the Lycée de Nations International School in Geneva, I introduced the concept of an adventure week for middle and high school students, a week of challenging outdoor pursuits (to be held near the beginning of the school year), which would help bind both students and staff together. That had proved a great success in Switzerland and I wanted to repeat that idea at Southbank. During the school's first year, however, we were so stretched that we could not manage it. But we did organise a long weekend at Upnor in Kent, a weekend of outdoor pursuits such as archery, orienteering and horse riding, and this was the precursor of what we thereafter called Discovery Week. In the early years all students and all staff (no excuses) went away together for a week in September. The venues varied from the Lake District to Wales to Devon, but the purpose remained the same. It was a time to share and work together, to get to know each other (and oneself), to face and overcome physical challenges and to develop leadership skills. As the school grew it became increasingly difficult to send everyone away together; so the school tended to be split by age groups. Furthermore, some staff found reasons not to go. So the idea of binding the whole school together was lost; nevertheless, Discovery Week remained a useful tool for getting to know at least part of the community and for fulfilling its other objectives.

So successful was the concept that a second Discovery Week was introduced in the spring. This was to be more skills-based, an opportunity to learn a new skill or to follow some special interest. Examples were music, drama, creative writing, horse riding, even cookery. These trips cut across the age groups and their quality depended largely on the ingenuity of individual teachers who arranged them. Later, foreign trips were added to the menu.

Over the years the Discovery Weeks became more formulaic. We tended to use the same centres year after year. They became easier to organise and also became shorter – the week had shrunk to four days. Although they continued to be a valuable part of a Southbank education, I felt they had lost some of the sparkle, excitement and spontaneity of the often last-minute and nerve-wracking arrangements that previously took place. Andy Burt, who was for many years in charge of modern languages at Southbank (he's now in Hong Kong), was particularly good at keeping us guessing until the last moment about the details of his Discovery Weeks. Because he wanted the students to be involved in making the arrangements, so much was left to the last minute. Yet in the end his trips were always among the most successful, largely because the students could say, "We did it ourselves."

The annual Suzuki concert given by the combined Hampstead and Kensington campuses is one of the highlights of the year. The sight (not to mention the sound!) of more than three hundred primary-aged children playing the violin or cello together is a thrilling one. And it is not all 'Twinkle Twinkle Little Star'. Ensembles and soloists play a range of music of varying complexity. Nobody who was present at the concert in the Hippodrome (then the home of the BBC Concert Orchestra) will forget the magical cello playing of Ari Evan, aged eight. He entranced every one with his assured playing. I also invited Ari to play at the high school graduation. At first he was reluctant to do so as it meant missing a Little League baseball game. Fortunately, however, he eventually accepted the invitation and again thrilled the audience with his bravura performance. Ari has gone on to study the cello at the Juilliard in New York.

International Day or International Night (depending on the campus or the era) became one of the enduring and most enjoyable events on the Southbank calendar. The concept is simple: everyone brings a dish of food from his or her home country, the food is laid out on tables and everyone helps themselves. The result is probably the best spread in London. In some years refinements and entertainment were added, but the basic concept did not change. After the opening of the Hampstead campus, the event was a combined Kensington/Hampstead affair, but it subsequently became an individual campus event. I suppose the growth of the school made the separation inevitable, but that's a pity nonetheless as it was one of the few opportunities for Southbank families from all campuses to get together and feel part of a larger whole.

When Hampstead opened, the lovely space that is now the Sandra LaRocca library (named after a parent who gave tirelessly of her time to set it up) was crying out to be used. Jane Treftz and a former Southbank parent, Manon Kanaroglou, came up with the idea of creating a children's art gallery. I was privileged to be at the first meeting that resulted in the establishment of the London International Gallery of Children's Art. It was an ambitious project and there was no certainty that it would succeed. The idea was that children's art from around the world would be displayed.

Bosnia had been devastated by a vicious civil war. We thought we would provide art supplies to a school and home for refugee children and then display their works at the new gallery. So the Southbank community, from both campuses, raised money through their annual sponsored charity walk to buy art supplies. These were then sent to the refugee home in Croatia. We were also able to hire a local artist to work with the children. Paula Ellis, a parent and art teacher at Southbank, made what was then a perilous journey to select and bring back the children's paintings. That resulted in the most moving exhibition called Homelandlessness, which was opened by Martin Bell, the famous foreign correspondent who had covered the war in the former Yugoslavia. Most of the paintings depicted the children's perceptions of the war and were often harrowing to look at.

The growth of Southbank Hampstead meant that LIGCA had to find a new home. Jane Treftz had the brilliant idea of asking the developers of the O2 Centre, which was just being built in Finchley Road, if they would donate space to the gallery. Part of the O2's planning obligations was the provision of space for community use and they kindly agreed to make available, free of charge, a lovely space which became the London International Gallery of Children's Art. LIGCA has become a charitable trust in its own right, but the links with Southbank remained strong, with several staff and parents on the Board of Trustees, notably Jane Treftz and Mary Langford who have jointly chaired the board. Two Southbank parents, Paola Longobardi and Barbara Lascelles, have remained highly supportive of LIGCA. Like the Hampstead campus, the London International Gallery of Children's Art was officially opened by Glenda Jackson, the MP for the area and at that time a minister in the government. There have been many memorable exhibitions at the gallery from around the world, including the Sahel, China, Mexico and South Africa. The gallery subsequently moved to Highgate and is now seeking a new home. Meanwhile it has an online presence and a very active outreach programme in partnership with other organisations such as schools and embassies. Their website (ligca.org) is well worth exploring.

One December, Marj, André and I went to Goa for Christmas and New Year. We stayed at Cidade de Goa, a lovely hotel which was really a self-contained resort. Although we made a few excursions out of the hotel we spent most of our time either sampling the delicious food or laying about on deckchairs or hammocks. As holiday reading I had brought with me *Liberation Management* by the management guru Tom Peters. As I was reading I became increasingly excited by his ideas on flat management. I developed an idea for implementing this at Southbank. On my return to London I set about doing just that. This, I thought, was entirely in keeping with the egalitarian ethos on which Southbank was founded.

How wrong I was! Those who then held posts of responsibility, such as heads of departments, were outraged at their loss of status (even though we promised no financial loss). In a few months the plan collapsed and we reverted to a more traditional hierarchy: flatter than most schools, admittedly, but hierarchical nevertheless.

It was a salutary lesson. Change works only after wide consultation and consent, or at least consensus. Of course I already knew that, but had been carried away by my own enthusiasm.

At the end of the school's first year there were twelve shareholders, the five founders plus the rest of the full-time staff. This was in keeping with the idea of the school as a cooperative. But the turbulent events that led to the departure of John Marberry and the resignation of several teachers (some as a direct consequence of these events) resulted in shrinkage of the shareholder base. By the end of the second year, in addition to myself, only Steve Bailey, Lesley Milton, Nigel Hughes and Janet Kuehn remained on the board. Brit Warren, who founded the Scandinavian Studies Department, also came on board for a couple of years. We had by then realised that the automatic granting of equal shares to all employees after a year at the school was a very messy structure. Gradually, the shareholder base shrank until, by the time we moved to Notting Hill, only Steve, Lesley, Nigel and I remained. We recognised that this was too small a base and invited several staff members – Andy Burt, Jane Treftz and Ben Joseph – to join the board. We subsequently also invited them to become shareholders, but only Ben took up the offer. (Jane later became a shareholder in the Hampstead school, which was set up as a separate company.)

When Steve Bailey returned to the United States, Ben took over as the school's Finance Director. This turned out to be a crucial and timely appointment. Ben got to grips with the school's finances. He discovered that the school was haemorrhaging cash. By detecting the source of what can only be described as embezzlement, Ben saved the school from almost certain bankruptcy. He put in place new systems and controls, proper budgeting and accounting procedures, which have ensured that Southbank has been in good financial health ever since.

In July 2001 I retired from the post of headmaster of Southbank International School, a post I had held for twenty-one years. There was no pressure on me to retire, but I had promised Marj that I would retire at the age of sixty-five. Although I had plenty of energy left and was still brimming with ideas, I felt that the school would benefit from fresh leadership.

My shares were redistributed among the other directors (Nigel and Ben at Kensington, plus Jane at Hampstead). Because Kensington was now owned by two equal shareholders, I retained a 2% share in order to ensure that any future deadlock could be broken if necessary.

I knew that my shares were significantly undervalued when I sold them, but I also knew that the school could not afford to pay out the real value of the shares. When the school was eventually sold to Cognita five years later, the price achieved was twelve times the valuation on which the board had based my buy-out. Nigel and Jane both recognised this and agreed to pass on to me about 10% of what they received from the sale. I am very grateful to them for this gesture, not simply because the extra money was useful but because it recognised my contribution to the success of Southbank.

We thought long and hard about my replacement as headmaster. The dilemma we faced was that any outside appointee would in effect be employed by those (Nigel, Ben and Jane) who would be under him or her in the school's hierarchy. In the end we decided on an internal appointment and Nigel Hughes became the new head of Southbank, a job he did effectively until the school was sold.

Of course this meant that a replacement had to be found for Nigel's old job as principal of the high school. I had encouraged Gwen Martinez, the school's guidance counsellor and IB coordinator, to apply. In the end, however, we appointed an outsider. This proved to be a bad appointment which we all later regretted. It also led to a strained relationship with Gwen, who naturally felt aggrieved that she had not been appointed. It took some years before this relationship was healed.

Some thoughts on education and Southbank's future

For Southbank to remain Southbank, there are some essential things that have to be maintained. One is to have a climate in the school in which people feel reasonably free to express themselves in various ways. Students at a certain level must be able to be themselves but I think that applies to teachers as well. They need to be encouraged to try things. There needs to be a climate of innovation in the school. New ideas must not be seen as threats. I don't mean that things should be embraced simply because they are new but I think a readiness to try something new is important in any organisation. This means a willingness to take some risks. Without being prepared to take risks, you actually stagnate. So I have always encouraged people to come up with ideas. Whatever the idea, e.g. a course, a new method, a trip, I liked to let them have a go at it. Sometimes it worked and sometimes it didn't. If it didn't work, that was fine, as long as every attempt didn't fail. I think that's part of the climate I definitely hope will be maintained.

I think administration and leadership are different. A book I read many years ago had a lot of influence on my own thinking. It was called *Up the Organisation* and was written by Robert Townsend, the man who took over Avis and came up with the slogan 'We're only number two. So we try harder'. It was quite a slim volume but a brilliant book on management.

He quotes from the Chinese philosopher Lao-tzu, who said that there were three types of leaders. The first is one that the people fear and they work because of their fear. The second type is slightly better, one that the people love, and they do things because they love him. But with the best type of leadership the people say, "We did it ourselves."

"A leader is best when people scarcely know he exists. Not so good when they kindly obey and acclaim him. Worse when they despise him. Fail to honour people, they fail to honour you. But of a good leader, who talks little, when his work is done and his aim fulfilled, they will say, 'We did it ourselves'" (Lao-tzu).

Townsend also said, "A leader is not an administrator who loves to run others, but someone who carries water for his people so that they can get on with their jobs." Providing that type of leadership was always my aspiration.

What is more, it is also a form of management. I think if you see management as simply being administration, you end up with paper shuffling. Of course, you do need to be organised, and if you're not you need someone with you who is. You should be aware of your own weaknesses. If you can't resolve them yourself then you need people who can complement what you do. That's another thing I always tried to do (though I am not saying I always succeeded), namely, to find people who had complementary strengths, not looking for clones of myself, which would have just compounded my weaknesses!

I expected teachers to be professionals. I worked on the assumption that they were going to do a good job, not on the assumption that they needed to be checked all the time. So to a very large extent, unless they proved otherwise, I trusted them to do their jobs. On the whole, that's what they did do. They seemed to respond well to somebody having high expectations of them and letting them get on with the job without undue interference. My attitude to students was no different.

Of course, from time to time people would let me down, just as I would from time to time let them down. Such imperfections are just part of human nature.

A school plays only a part – an important part but still only a part – in a child's development. The family is by far the most important influence. A school must recognise its limitations and work with the family to help a child reach his or her full potential.

One way is to create within the school a harmonious community. If we do that I am convinced that such values will be carried over into later life. And even if they are not, at least students will have had a happy experience while they were at school. It also allows students to feel comfortable and that in turn leads to greater self-confidence, one of the most important attributes in life.

I think bigotry is what I'm most opposed to. It can take lots of forms, such as racism and intolerance of the beliefs of others. Rejection of others because of physical or mental disability or because of their sexuality is also a form of bigotry which I feel very strongly about. At Southbank I had to expel very few students, but in nearly every case the student concerned was involved in bullying. I do recall one case where a student punched a local tramp who was always drunk but harmless, but who on this occasion asked the student for money. The student's aggressive response was totally disproportionate, nor would he recognise the gravity of his conduct. Despite the pleas of his mother, I felt he could not continue at Southbank.

When the school was founded there were some ideas which overrode all others. The first was that Southbank (or AIS as it then was) would be an international school. The second was that Southbank would be a democratic community. Thirdly, Southbank would be a school without walls, making use of London as the classroom. Fourthly, the curriculum would meet individual needs.

From these principles flow a number of others:

As an international school, Southbank should respect every individual, no matter what his or her background or beliefs. The curriculum should reflect the international nature of the school, eschewing narrow national points of view. The international student body should be a cause for celebration, not complaint. Recognising language as the key to communication, the school should provide a language-rich environment. This means providing opportunities for students to study any foreign language, their native tongue and the language of instruction (i.e. English). As part of one world we should reach out to and help those less fortunate than ourselves.

Although experience taught us that a school cannot operate as a completely democratic community with all decisions taken, after open discussion, by majority vote of the staff, students and parents (this method was often in conflict with other core values such as fairness and tolerance), nevertheless, in the structure which is developed, some important elements should be retained. These include wide consultation, seeking consensus, listening to the views of others, willingness to change. Community spirit is an essential part of the democratic process; so responsibility (and accountability) for one's actions and responsibility towards others should form part of the ethos. Each member of the Southbank community should be empowered to make decisions and expected to make choices.

As a school without walls, Southbank should be open to the outside world and to new ideas. Innovation should be welcomed as an exciting challenge, not rejected as a burdensome nuisance. It should give rein to the creativity and imagination of those who form its community. Southbank should be a community not of teachers and taught, but of learners and learners. By using London as the classroom, the school would have at its disposal all the facilities of this great city.

As a school meeting individual needs, Southbank should be flexible. This means finding out each student's learning style, interests and aptitudes. The culture should be one of high expectations based on the belief that every student can succeed. In Queen Victoria's words, we are "not interested in the possibilities of defeat". Educating the whole person should be the school's aim.

Southbank should be a place where integrity, fairness and decency are the norm.

Good exam results are important, for they are the key to entry to the next stage of education, but they are by no means the most important part of a student's education at Southbank. Grades and exams deal only with those bits of education that are easy to measure. The really important bits relate to our development as human beings: our empathy, our creativity, our imagination, the way we treat each other, our contribution to the future.

As Albert Einstein said, "Imagination is more important than knowledge. Knowledge is limited. Imagination encircles the world."

In The *Ascent of Man*, Bronowski said, "It is important that students bring a certain ragamuffin, barefoot irreverence to their studies; they are not here to worship what is known, but to question it."

Fostering the imagination, developing an inquiring mind, taking risks, being creative – these were always fundamental aims at Southbank. I fully concur with the great Swiss educator Jean Piaget's statement that "the principal goal of education is to create (people) who are capable of doing new things, not simply of repeating what other generations have done – (people) who are creative, inventive and discoverers."

The international nature of Southbank is particularly important. When we watch with horror and a feeling of helplessness events such as civil wars and the slaughter of innocents, we may believe there is nothing we can do about it. In the short term, apart from protesting and contributing financially, there is indeed little we can do to alter the situation, but in the longer term we can make a difference. And that difference is in the way we treat each other. In an international community such as Southbank, it doesn't matter whether you are an Arab or Jew,

Sunni or Shia, Serb or Albanian, Indian or Pakistani, Tutsi or Hutu, black or white, we have an exceptional opportunity to treat each other as fellow humans.

George Bernard Shaw once remarked that, "patriotism is your conviction that this country is superior to all others because you were born in it." While I don't fully share his cynicism, there is more than a grain of truth in this. When we discriminate against others because of their nationality, their religion, their colour, their gender, their sexuality, we are simply proclaiming our own superiority and revealing our own ignorance and prejudice. By overcoming such shortcomings we can indeed influence future events.

A school becomes international not simply because it has students of different nationalities. It becomes international when we respect each other regardless of origin, when we open our minds to new ideas. We can still be proud of our own national identity, hold to our own beliefs, but we recognise that, though others may have different beliefs, we respect them nonetheless.

A former Southbank student, Cynthia Harvey, who was in Southbank Hampstead's first eighth-grade class, expressed it beautifully. (Cynthia later graduated from Brown University.) This extract has appeared in some Southbank publications, and I am grateful to Jane Treftz, Hampstead's founding Principal, for providing me with the text. Cynthia has given me permission to reproduce her essay. This is what she said:

For my intermediate years I found myself in London at a tiny institution called Southbank International School. I was in its maiden graduation class. As common wisdom dictates, adolescence is an extremely difficult time in any culture. Perhaps no one knows this better than those eight kids in that class.

Our situations were distinct, but similar. English was the native language of three members of the class. I was the only American; my best friend was a Japanese girl who spoke very little English. Most of us had not been in the country for more than a few months, all of us were scared, and a few of us were petrified. Our teacher had just returned from Irian Jaya, so he was in a similar state of mind. In those circumstances, we were alike. In nearly every other, we were different.

The Swedish boy was the class crush. The Japanese boy was the class clown. The Canadian was a science-oriented former cheerleader and Christian fundamentalist. I was an outspoken aspiring author who suddenly found herself wordless. The Turkish boy was obnoxious. The Portuguese girl had a beautiful smile.

That class was my second family. Having previously attended the local public elementary that crammed 37 kids into a 20-person classroom, I suddenly discovered the energy that could come from a group of eight totally different young adults. What I learned from them was more important than anything else I learned in middle school; we could not always communicate, but we taught each other. We wandered around London. We took class trips to castles, moors, and museums. Outside of school, we commiserated, made sushi rolls, and played baseball. Not one of us matched.

Southbank did not harp on diversity, so we never understood the gravity of the differences between us, the need for cultural awareness, or the importance of taking care not to offend.

No one told us that we should treat each other any differently than we had treated our friends at home and no one made us look at the cultural backgrounds that separated us. Because of that, we were able to behave naturally with each other, without thought to the political or social boundaries that separated us. We were a class of eight students, far from home, who needed each other.

Just like everyone else I am a collection, not only of personal traits but a collection of experiences. What I have seen, where I have been, whom I have known, and what I have done make me what I am. With every experience, I become richer. My awareness becomes deeper. I am myself because I write, I act, and I hold myself to high standards. I am myself because of those seven other kids at Southbank, who taught me *about themselves, their countries and their philosophies, without really trying. I am myself because of Yukiko, Arif, Karina, and Toshi, and everyone else whose simple presence has unknowingly shaped me.*

In 1995 we sold our house in Wimbledon where we had lived for eighteen years. It was too large for just the two of us. Furthermore, with Southbank's acquisition of its Hampstead campus, I felt that the commute was too long. It was a time of IRA threats, and the tubes would be stopped and stations evacuated so often that travelling by underground had become increasingly unpleasant.

Our house was sold within a few days to the first person who viewed it. We moved into a small furnished flat near Marble Arch and began our search for a new home. A few months later we found a delightful flat in Maida Vale where we lived for the next nine years. It was situated about halfway between Southbank's Kensington and Hampstead campuses, less than ten minutes' drive from each.

In the summer before Nathalie went to boarding school we spent a fortnight in the then Yugoslavia. While there we drove across the border for a one-day visit to Venice. We found a restuarant where they served whole lobsters. We all enjoyed a lobster each, but my daughter Nathalie just loved them and wanted more.

Looking at the price, which was just a few hundred lire '*a l'etto*', I agreed. So she had a few more lobsters and I think we all had seconds. In my ignorance and arrogance (after all, I had studied some Italian!) I was sure that a '*a l'etto*' meant 'each'. It sounds like it, doesn't it? Just a few hundred lire each, well, why not eat more? When it came to settling the bill I discovered that '*a l'etto*' was the Italian for 'per 100 grams'! We had eaten several kilos of lobster and the total bill came to well over £150, a fortune for us at the time, and far in excess of the cash I had with me. Fortunately, my credit card, which I rarely used in those days, managed to cover the bill.

Retirement

At the time of my retirement my mother was visiting us from South Africa. This visit should have taken place a year earlier in order for her to attend André's and Nathalie's wedding. Unfortunately, she had fallen very badly in a cinema in Cape Town and was scarcely able to move for several months. The healing process took a very long time.

It was 23 June 2001, my sixty-fifth birthday. Term had just ended and the weather was particularly hot. Marj, Mom and I had spent the day with André and Nathalie. I was pretty tired and just wanted to spend the evening at home, but the rest of the family wanted to go out for a meal. Reluctantly, I put on a pair of long trousers after wearing shorts all day. We decided to eat at the O2 in Hampstead, a restaurant and entertainment complex. While there, Marj suggested that we show Mom the London International Gallery of Children's Art (a gallery founded by Southbank International School). The gallery was on the top floor of the complex, and as we made our way to the lift we could hear a lot of noise and laughter coming from the large hall on the first floor. Marj insisted that we look inside to see what was going on. I objected, as I did not want to intrude on a private party. But she literally pushed me through the double doors into the hall, and there inside were hundreds of Southbank staff, both present and past, together with their spouses and partners. It was a surprise dinner party for my retirement. I was really overwhelmed by it all, as I had absolutely no idea that this event had been organised.

I had already had various farewell parties, but this one was truly special. Most memorably, Michele Key, the school secretary at Kensington, dressed as Marilyn Monroe and sang Happy Birthday in a fine imitation of Marilyn's tribute to President Kennedy. At that event I felt a great deal of warmth and affection towards me, feelings which I certainly reciprocated.

For many years we arranged most of our holidays through exchanging homes with families abroad. In retirement, the frequency of these exchanges increased, enabling us to visit countries around the world. Apart from cost, one of the great advantages of a house swap is that it enables you to live as a local, a totally different experience from staying in a hotel.

Immediately after I retired we arranged a house swap with a Norwegian couple who had a flat in Fuengirola in Spain. A few months earlier Marj and I had visited Spain with the intention of buying a property. Rather rashly we put down a deposit on an apartment that had not yet been built, with the promise that it would be part of an 'urbanizacion' which would include gardens, swimming pools, shops, a spa and other leisure facilities. It was a risk, but in fact the developers fulfilled all their promises. The Reserva del Higueron near Benalmadena is today a magnificent and beautiful complex, apparently unaffected by the general downturn in Spain's property market.

Our stay in Fuengirola was for the purpose of viewing the progress of the construction of our flat. One afternoon (it was 11 September 2001) I turned on the television, and was surprised to see what I assumed was a movie, a most unusual occurrence on CNN. After watching for a few minutes I became aware that this was a real event. It was the destruction of the Twin Towers in New York. The sight of planes crashing into these two iconic buildings is one I will never forget. The Norwegian couple who were staying in our flat in London were so upset that they immediately flew back to Norway.

Once our flat in Spain was ready, it was our intention to

spend the winter months there and the summer in London. But Emilie's birth in May 2002 meant that we no longer wanted to be away from London for such long periods. We wanted to spend as much time as possible with our first grandchild.

André's wife Nathalie had embarked on another law degree, and this meant that we would look after Emilie every morning while Nathalie was attending classes. This was a great joy to us and helped develop a strong bond with Emilie. Later, when Emilie began nursery school we picked her up every day and looked after her until André fetched her after work.

When André and Nathalie moved from their small flat in Willesden to a larger flat in Herne Hill this arrangement was no longer possible. Of course, when they later moved to France (just over the border from Geneva where André worked) we saw Emilie and our two other grandchildren, Emma and Léo, much less frequently. However, the three children do stay with us from time to time and we are able to visit them in France. We are grateful that André and Nathalie have always encouraged the children to maintain strong bonds with their grandparents.

After a few years the flat in Spain was starting to become a millstone around our necks. Of course we enjoyed our holidays there, as did friends and relations, but we almost felt obliged to go back to the same place all the time and found that we often spent much of our time on trying to improve the property. So we decided to put it up for sale. For many months there was just no movement. We sometimes used our flat in Spain for house swaps. One day we received a call from a couple staying in the flat that someone had knocked on the door and asked if the flat was for sale. The person making the inquiry was Spanish. I flew out to Spain and a successful sale was negotiated. Although we were sorry to bid farewell to the Reserva del Higueron, this came as a great relief. It was also timely, as shortly thereafter the bottom fell out of the Spanish property market.

Nathalie

Nineteen eighty-nine was our *annus horribilis*. On the night of the spring equinox, 21 March, our beloved daughter Nathalie died. She had been in intensive care for nearly two weeks and had finally succumbed to the effects of her ruined lungs. She was just nineteen.

Until the age of thirteen, Nathalie had been an almost model child. She worked hard at school and always tried to please. Of course, there had been a few ups and downs. When we took over Greystones Nursery School in Stroud, Nathalie, who was just three at the time, found it difficult to adjust to being a member of a nursery class. Greystones was, after all, her home and she could not see why she was not allowed to be with her parents whenever she wished. This problem was solved by enrolling her in another nursery where she was quite happy.

When I resigned from the American Community School in 1979, Nathalie took her transfer to Wimbledon Chase Middle School in her stride, quickly making many local friends. Although the quality of the education there was pretty modest, Nathalie was a conscientious pupil and did reasonably well.

On completion of middle school, at the age of thirteen Nathalie joined Southbank International School. On the whole she made good progress, but she was greatly influenced by some of her more social fellow students. She was always pushing the boundaries a little further out. Relations at home became very difficult; there were constant arguments, particularly between

Nathalie and Marj. At times things became almost unbearable. Nathalie was also embarrassed by having her father as headmaster of the school she attended. One day, after a performance in the school of *A Midsummer Night's Dream*, in which she had a part, she was extremely rude and confrontational on our way home. I thought it might be good for her and for all of us if she went to boarding school, as both Marj and I had done. This proved to be one of the worst decisions of my life.

After some research we chose St Christopher School in Letchworth. I liked the philosophy and ethos of the school, and after visiting the place even Nathalie was quite positive about going there. During the summer prior to her starting at St Chris, we spent a couple of weeks in Yugoslavia. Nathalie was obviously apprehensive about going to boarding school and we nearly changed our minds. Would that we had.

When we arrived at St Chris at the beginning of the school year we were dismayed to find that the delightful houseparents we had previously met had left the school and had been replaced by another man, whom we found to be pompous and unsympathetic. This was a bad start for Nathalie.

However, Nathalie seemed to settle quite quickly into her new school. Pupils were allowed to come home every few weekends, and Nathalie seemed quite upbeat on these occasions, even bringing some of her new friends home.

Unfortunately, however, she had begun to experiment with marijuana, but we were unaware of this. The mother of one of her friends had noticed that her own daughter was being sucked into drugs and so withdrew her from St Chris. How I wish we had done the same, though it may already have been too late.

I do not blame St Chris for the fact that Nathalie was smoking marijuana. After all, I know that many students at Southbank were also experimenting with drugs. Equally, there were many students in both schools (indeed, in all schools) that managed to resist the lure of drugs. Alas, Nathalie was not one of them. No, the reason that I regret our decision to send Nathalie to boarding school is that we lost the ability to influence her decisions.

Nathalie had joined St Chris in Year 11, the year in which the GCSE exams were taken. This made the academic programme difficult for her, as she had not received the preparation given to other students. She did, however, do well in art and drama, exhibiting considerable talent in both. So, although her GCSE results were insufficient, she was admitted to the sixth form, taking art, drama and English.

One weekend, there occurred an event from which she never recovered. She had been invited overnight to the home of a Southbank friend. They went out with two male acquaintances of her friend, and while the girl and one of the men were out of the car, Nathalie was raped by the other man. She returned to St Chris the next day as arranged and only when she came home the following weekend did she tell us of her ordeal. For some reason, Marj found it difficult to accept what had happened and was inclined to blame Nathalie for the rape. I was more understanding. We called the Rape Crisis Centre, but got no help from them. I wish we had called the Samaritans, which I discovered only later would have been a good source of help.

Nathalie did not want the matter reported to the police, and we felt we had to respect her wishes. Today, victims of rape are treated more sympathetically by the police, who often have specially trained officers to assist, but at the time, girls who reported rape were often blamed or not believed. I think Nathalie was (with justification) afraid of the police interrogation and subsequent court ordeal.

I borrowed several books from the library on the subject of rape in order to understand its effects and how to deal with its aftermath. After the initial shock, Marj came around and provided Nathalie with a lot of support. We sought help from a couple of psychologists.

Although Nathalie seemed to be coping, I believe that we

can date her downfall from that event. At the end of the term, with her agreement and that of the school, we pulled her out of St Chris. Despite an excellent performance in a school play, her grades had slipped and her drug habit had increased.

She did not want to go to any other school and was rather indifferent about looking for work. At last she found a part-time job as a waitress in Pizza Hut in Wimbledon. However, she decided that she wanted a career in modelling. Thanks to Mrs Bolt, a parent at Southbank who ran a modelling agency, Nathalie had a beautiful portfolio, which Mrs Bolt distributed to her clients. But modelling is a waiting game, and rejections are frequent. You have to be ready at a moment's notice. While Nathalie was at the Glastonbury Festival she was called by Vivienne Westwood – the only call she received in several weeks. But there was no way to contact her (mobile phones did not exist). So she missed a good opportunity.

She had met a man named Mark in a local Wimbledon pub. He was in his late twenties, an unemployed drug addict. Nathalie fell for him and was completely obsessed by him. This was extremely worrying. To encourage Nathalie to live at home, we had converted our living room into a self-contained studio flat with its own kitchenette, toilet and shower, but after a few months she decided to move out and live with Mark.

Under his malign influence she dropped out of nearly everything, just occasionally visiting us. By this time she was well into drugs, including heroin. She had at least one miscarriage. We were at our wit's end and did not know how to deal with her. We tried tough love, but all to no avail.

Towards the end of 1988 she came home at last and asked for help. We managed to get her into a drug rehabilitation centre at St George's hospital, but she left after a few days and went back to Mark. However, a little later she came back to us.

She was recovering so well that she agreed to return to Southbank for the last two terms of that school year in order to obtain a high school diploma. She was by then nineteen, older than most of her classmates, but that was not an unusual situation at Southbank.

Things were going quite well when she discovered that she was pregnant. Should she have the baby? It would have had a drug addict as a father and a (hopefully) recovering addict as a mother. Marj, in keeping with her Catholic upbringing, was opposed to abortion. I took a more neutral stance, but we both agreed that we would support Nathalie whatever her decision. I took her to St Thomas' Hospital for counselling, after which she decided to have an abortion. This was carried out at the Elizabeth Garrett Anderson Hospital for Women, where she was given further opportunities to change her mind, but she decided to go ahead.

As with the rape, I had no idea of the effect of an abortion on a woman. Nathalie was certainly affected and became quite depressed. She returned to school, naturally unable to speak of her experience to anyone. I arranged for her to have further counselling, which she seemed to find helpful.

However, one evening she went out and did not come back. We were very worried. Early the next morning she appeared, staggering up the garden path. She had been dropped off or, rather, dumped by some 'friends'. (Mark was not involved on this occasion.)

I have to confess that my reaction when she arrived in what seemed a drunken state was one of extreme anger. "I'm wasted," she said, "but I only had two beers." With that she almost collapsed. I called 999 and was told to lay her in the recovery position. The ambulance came within minutes and took her to St George's Hospital in Tooting. There she was sedated, taken to intensive care and hooked up to a ventilator.

The doctor explained that it appeared she had inhaled her own vomit. This led swiftly to pneumonia. The ventilator was needed to give her lungs the chance to recover. She had what is called Mendelson's syndrome, an acute pneumonia caused by regurgitation of stomach contents and aspiration of chemical material, usually gastric juices.

Before she was sedated, Nathalie was asked whether it would be all right to test her for HIV and apparently she said no. This was a grave error, for a few days later one of the options considered was a lung transplant. However, because Nathalie had taken heroin by injection, the specialist hospital contacted by St George's would not consider her for a transplant without an HIV test. And because Nathalie had earlier said she did not want such a test the hospital would not go against her wishes even though we asked them to do so. Two days before she died, the hospital finally agreed to carry out the test. Only after she died were the test results received: she was not HIV-positive.

During the entire ten days that Nathalie was in ITU she was sedated, except for a few minutes when she was given a sheet of paper and a pencil. She scribbled the letter M, then collapsed again. Was she asking for Mum, who was standing right next to her, or for Mark, a principal architect of her destruction? Or did she intend to write something else altogether different?

Throughout her stay in ITU, apart from brief intervals, either Marj or I stayed with Nathalie, often talking or reading to her. We had been told that sedated patients can often hear what is said. We of course also had to ensure that André was cared for.

On the final day, I had gone to work. Marj called me in the afternoon and said I should come to the hospital. I was full of foreboding. That evening, Nathalie's condition deteriorated. In addition to the nurses, only a junior doctor was on duty. At about ten o'clock there was a lot of activity around Nathalie's bed. Nathalie's other organs had shut down and she had died. Would she have been saved if a more senior doctor or consultant had been on duty that evening? We will never know. I do not want to be critical of the hospital staff, who all tried their best to save Nathalie and looked after her with such care. But I cannot help feeling that there was a lack of expertise in her treatment.

No one can describe the feeling of emptiness and desolation when you lose a child. It remains with you always. Not a day passes without my reliving the events of that day. Nathalie was my child and I had failed to protect her. I know she was unlucky. Many children go astray for a while, but they get through this period and develop into responsible adults. I was always sure that would happen to Nathalie, but instead she had the misfortune to inhale her own vomit and die.

I cannot say that we handled her death well. Of course we went through all the motions. Avi Chandiok, a good friend and the school's accountant, kindly arranged the funeral, which was held in the North-East Surrey cemetery in Morden. Hundreds of people, many from Southbank and St Christopher, attended the cremation.

I spoke at her funeral as follows:

"My dearest Marjorie, my dearest André, dear family and friends, this is probably the hardest job I've ever had to do. I never expected to have to be present at my own child's funeral. But here I am, here we are. I only hope I can get through what I want to say, because I owe it to you, Nat.

"Just look at how many people have come to your funeral, my darling. It shows how much you are loved, and have always been loved.

"When you were lying desperately ill in St George's Hospital, so many of your friends, so many of our friends – and that's the same thing – came to see you, to talk to you, to hold your hand and stroke your brow, to tell you how much we love you. You couldn't answer, but I know you heard us and were aware of our presence.

"On the fourth day the doctors concluded that you were gravely ill. The sister thought you would die that night, but you hung on there for another eight days. You really tried, you really fought, and I am sure that the support you got from all of us, your family and friends, helped you in your struggle for life.

Every moment then was precious. We were never closer, never more intimate. Those late nights, when I whispered my love and read you my favourite poems, were some of the most bittersweet experiences of my life.

"Mum and I were with you when you died. Painful though it was and painful though it always will be, I am glad we were there and that you did not die alone. And a great part of me died with you.

"Nineteen and a half years ago I had the overwhelming joy and privilege of being present at your birth. As you emerged with your long dark hair I thought you were the most beautiful of God's creatures. I still think you are.

"On entering this chapel we heard the music of the songbird. You were also a lovely bird that for a while lost her way. But you were back on course and were winging your way to dry land when you fell just short of the shore.

"To change the image: it is an ancient custom to sacrifice a lamb at the onset of spring. You, my darling, are that lamb. You died on the equinox, giving birth to spring. A true Agnus Dei.

"You were a child of two continents, born on a third, a child of two religions, a child of two cultures, a child of today, a symbol of our common humanity.

"When a young person dies, it leaves you asking, 'Why, Why?' It seems impossibly cruel to end a life so close to its beginning. And when it's your own child, it is quite beyond understanding. Yet if death is the end then life can have no meaning. So, though we are going to miss you terribly in these coming days and months and years, my darling, I believe that one day we shall be reunited. Till then, my sweet, au revoir and God bless you. Thank you for your sweetness and the tender memories. Thank you for being you.

Is life a boon?
If so, it must befall
That death whene'er he call
Must call too soon.

The cemetery is a beautiful, peaceful place. While we lived in Wimbledon I visited it often, at least once a week. Now we go there two or three times a year, on Nathalie's birthday, on the anniversary of her death, and usually around Christmas. But in my thoughts she is always with me. The loss of our darling daughter is the most profound tragedy of my life.

The year after Nathalie's death I wanted to do something in her memory. I decided to become a Samaritan. The Samaritans provide a helpline for people who feel suicidal or indeed just need to talk about their problems. After undergoing a period of training I became a full-fledged Samaritan at the Putney branch, the nearest to our home in Wimbledon. The Samaritans are entirely non-judgmental, which very much suited my approach to life. Listening to people's problems, empathising with them, and knowing that sometimes you were able to help them face the future was a privilege, often harrowing but always rewarding.

Nathalie's death put a great strain on our marriage. I have read that the death of a child usually leads to marriage breakdown. At one point I was certainly ready to call it a day. It was only Marj's determination and commitment that saved our marriage, and of course I am grateful that she succeeded. As I write, we have been married for nearly fifty years. Despite ups and downs it is a relationship that has endured and has strengthened into an unbreakable bond.

Me

I have always had a rather placid and equable temperament. When I was doing the short business course while we were setting up Southbank International School, the tutor Ronnie Lessem gave us a personality test. My results alarmed him. He said that I was so laid back that if I ever reached a tipping point I would just snap and react violently.

Well, so far that has not happened. I have occasionally lost my temper, causing a minor ruckus, but in general I have great self-control. Probably too much, since my feelings are usually controlled behind an apparently benign mask. I do feel, very deeply, but I seldom show it.

In appearance, I have had a weight problem ever since my age reached double figures. Earlier photographs show a slim, even skinny boy with protruding ears and a large nose. A few years later the ears and nose remain the same, but the figure has become overweight.

Thus, when I went to boarding school at the age of thirteen, the combination of my surname and rotund appearance led naturally to the nickname of 'Tubby' - a moniker I did not lose until I started teaching at Churchill School in 1957, when none of my school friends were at hand.

Once, at the age of about fourteen, I was sitting in the back seat of a Lanchester driven by a friend of my mother's. She turned to my mother, who was sitting next to her, and said, "He's not at all good-looking, but he has a nice smile and that should be enough."

I don't know why her remark remains etched on my brain. At least I have not had any illusions about my looks. Yet I have been told many times that my smile, of which I am never conscious, seems to draw people into my confidence.

Children that I know, pupils that I've taught, friends and colleagues alike, have told me that my smile has given them reassurance, and many have opened up to me.

I hope I have never betrayed their confidence. I know I am a good listener, a trait that has stood me in good stead throughout my life and helped me in my role as a Samaritan for a number of years. I am able to keep a secret and have never felt the need to spread rumours.

I think it is because I listen before I speak and avoid judging people that I am sometimes perceived as rather wise, an attribution that is totally unjustified. Unjustified, too, is the perception that I am scholarly. I wish I were, but the fact is that I simply try to avoid displaying my ignorance.

Although I enjoy an occasional glass of wine with a meal, I have never been drunk. Perhaps this is related to my need always to be in control of myself. Nor have I ever smoked. Once when I was at Rhodes University I placed a cigarette in my mouth and struck a match with the intention of lighting it. Just the smell of sulphur dioxide from the match made me feel ill. So I never actually lit the cigarette. That sounds rather like Bill Clinton's claim that he never inhaled, but it's true!

I have always been tempted to take risks (not physical ones, I hasten to add). This can be seen as a thread running throughout my life: running a 'casino' at boarding school; venturing out at night to visit friends in another hostel at Guinea Fowl; giving up what was then considered a secure job in order to go abroad; resigning the headship of the Lycée des Nations in Geneva to move to the UK with a wife and child and no job; returning to Geneva again without the prospect of work; resigning from my position as principal of the American Community School with no job in sight; and, of course, risking all by setting up a school with no money.

Marj

As I write, Marj has been an integral part of my life for nearly fifty years. Despite some crises, most especially just after our daughter Nathalie's death, our marriage has survived.

Marj was a very beautiful young woman (in my eyes she still is). It was easy to fall in love with her, as I did.

Marj is very good at keeping in touch with both friends and family. She loves company and becomes very dejected when there is nobody around to talk to. Whereas I am diffident about meeting new people, Marj is gregarious and has no difficulty in talking to strangers.

She is a very caring person, as evidenced by her choosing to work in a residential care home for several years. In our block of flats, where most of the residents are elderly, she has befriended and helped many of them. On our floor lived a lovely couple, Norma and Willie de Haan. Willie had lost both his arms during the war in an accident in occupied Holland. Although nobody could be more positive than Willie, he had to rely on his wife for help with the most basic tasks of washing, dressing and going to the toilet. When Norma fell ill it was to Marj that Willie turned for help, and she responded magnificently, assisting with these tasks and with putting on and taking off his prostheses. (Sadly, both Norma and Willie died within a few weeks of each other.)

More recently, Marj set up a social club in our apartment complex where most residents scarcely know each other. Many of the residents here are alone (widowed or divorced), and Marj provided an opportunity for them to get together. She has also organised two garden parties, which have been hugely enjoyed by everyone.

Marj would, I believe, concede that she is quite hot-tempered and quick to judge. She is also easily hurt and offended. But these are small faults that I have learnt to accept. They do not affect the love that I have for her.

André

In his early years, André was a rather adventurous, mischievous child, though never malicious.

When we returned to the UK from Switzerland, we rented a bungalow in the pretty village of Bisley, about ten miles from our nursery school in Stroud. The house backed onto open fields, while the front was approached along a cul-de-sac. That was fortunate as André had a tendency to wander off as soon as he could walk.

André's early schooling at Dundonald Primary School and at Wimbledon Chase Middle School was far from satisfactory. The fact is that he was bored and unstimulated.

It was a great relief when he was at last able to join Southbank International School at the age of eleven. André was among the first students to join our newly established 'Junior High' class. There was certainly a transformation in his attitude to school and in the level of his academic achievements.

On only one occasion did he get into trouble. On a school trip to France, he and his friend Kim Oeser let off a stink bomb on the ferry from Calais to Dover, much to the chagrin and embarrassment of Jane Treftz, the teacher in charge of the trip. I think he was suspended for a couple of days.

André also took up the trombone. Because the school had no trombone teacher we found a teacher who lived a short drive from our house in Wimbledon. André made excellent progress on this instrument and was eventually admitted to the Surrey

Youth Orchestra. He and I also attended a trombone festival in Birmingham. I regret that he gave up the trombone when he later went to Japan.

As a young child, he adored his sister Nathalie and would follow her everywhere. The two of them once set up a stall on the pavement outside our house and tried to sell some of our old pots, pans and other kitchen utensils. Talk of the Young Apprentice!

Later, of course, when he entered his teens, their relationship changed, but a strong bond remained. So Nathalie's death when he was fifteen and she was nineteen affected him deeply. I think Marj and I were so consumed by our own grief that we failed to acknowledge the impact on André and, in the belief that we were protecting him, seldom talked to him about her death.

Earlier in the same year I had read about a scholarship that was being offered for a student to spend a year in Japan at the YMCA International School in Osaka. André had been learning Japanese for several months with the mother of a Southbank student. To encourage him, I attended the class as well, though I have to admit that he was a far better student than I was.

(As a curious aside André had originally wanted to learn Chinese. I had therefore tried to find him a Mandarin tutor prior to the offer of Japanese lessons given by the Southbank parent. Then one day I received a letter summoning me to a government office near Admiralty Arch. There, I was closely, even aggressively, questioned about one of the Chinese tutors I had contacted. Since I knew nothing about him I was dismissed and told never to speak of the meeting. This is the first time I have mentioned it and hopefully I am not in breach of any secrecy laws!)

We decided to apply for the Japanese scholarship and were very pleased that André was selected for the award. Nathalie's death could have stopped us from allowing him to go to Japan, but we decided that we did not want to prevent him from taking advantage of this exceptional opportunity.

So, in July 1989, after he had sat his GCSE exams, André and

I travelled to Japan in a rickety Aeroflot plane via Moscow. The food on board was abysmal. As a snack we were given a dried-up apple, which I suppose is still healthier than most airline food.

Although my mind was clouded by constant thoughts of Nathalie, my three weeks in Japan were fascinating. The culture seemed so different from anything I had experienced before. On the one hand everything is so modern and all the services work perfectly; on the other hand the sights, sounds and smells, the food, the customs and body language are unique to Japan.

André and I travelled quite widely in Japan, staying in a mixture of accommodation: dormitories, ryokan, business hotels with minute rooms, and some western-style hotels. One smart hotel in Hiroshima had a toilet which washed your bottom with warm water. We also visited an onsen (a kind of spa) where as gaijin (foreigners) we were not made to feel welcome. Whenever we entered the pool most of the other bathers got out!

Although we both liked Japanese food, just occasionally we longed for something familiar and would eat at McDonalds or Dunkin' Donuts.

The pupils at the YMCA International School in Osaka were all Japanese except for André and one Danish boy. It must have been rather overwhelming for André at first, but he seemed to cope extremely well. He lived with a lovely family, the Uedas. Originally, he was supposed to stay with them for just one term and then move to another family. He got on so well with the Uedas that they asked him to stay with them for the rest of the year. I will always be grateful to them for the way they cared for André.

When he returned to the UK the following summer, André was fluent in Japanese. He rejoined Southbank to do the two-year course leading to the International Baccalaureate. His IB results were good enough for him to gain entry to the School of Oriental and African Studies at London University to study Japanese and Law.

In his second year at SOAS, André shared a flat with a friend, Adam Lindemann, who was also studying Japanese and Law.

Together they set up a small business, providing Japanese visitors to London with helpful services, acting as guides and organisers. It was a simple concept which worked extremely well. Later, their attempt to expand the business by adding more complex services was less successful. But I was very pleased to note André's entrepreneurial spirit.

During a subsequent visit to Japan, when he was just nineteen, he met a young Frenchwoman, three years older than he. They seemed to have hit it off really well. Nathalie Clerc, as she was called, later became his wife and the mother of our three beautiful grandchildren. The coincidence that our daughter-in-law shares the same name as our daughter often jolts people.

After qualifying as a solicitor in London (she already had law degrees from France and Japan), Nathalie had a high-powered job in the legal department of a Japanese bank in London. Since moving to France Nathalie has set up her own highly successful law practice in Echenevex where they live. There is a constant demand for her services, particularly in the field of family law.

André has made a career in financial services. Much to our disappointment, he and Nathalie moved to France in 2007. He worked first for Barclays Bank and then for Schroders in Geneva, just across the border. This means that we do not see them or our grandchildren as often as we would like, but since both Marj and I are global nomads ourselves, we can hardly complain.

I could not have wished for a better son than André. He is straightforward and open-minded. He is an exceptionally devoted father, not only providing a good life for his family, but giving Emilie, Emma and Léo a lot of time. I am sure he is a good husband too.

Parents and step-parents

Until I was thirteen years old, nearly all my relationships revolved around my mother's large family. She was the youngest of thirteen children; so I was surrounded by aunts, uncles and cousins. This extended family was a great boon to an only child. We were in and out of each other's homes and always seemed to be welcome wherever we went. Half the family lived in Pretoria, the rest in Johannesburg. (Two exceptions: Auntie Mary lived in Fish Hoek near Cape Town, and Uncle Hymie, whom I do not think I ever met, lived in Rhodesia.) On Sundays most of the Pretoria family got together for lunch. Many of the Jo'burg relations came down to see us periodically or we would go by train to see them. In many ways it was an idyllic arrangement. I'm sure there were family rows, but I don't recall any. Mom seemed to get on wonderfully with her brothers and sisters, while my cousins provided me with just about all the friends I needed. Of course, I did have other friends, in particular Ian Spitz and Michael Kaplan who both attended CBC. And I've already mentioned Helen Bender and Shirley Jacobi.

Jeffrey Arnall, Auntie Faye's son, was the closest companion of my childhood. Because we lived together during the war, we grew up almost as brothers; and his sister Rhona, four years older than I, was a great role model for both of us.

Then at the age of thirteen, after Mom's attempted suicide, everything changed. I was sent to live with my father and his second wife Stella in Umvuma, a pinprick of a town in the middle of Southern Rhodesia. There, Dad had bought a small hotel (the Falcon Hotel), which he gradually extended and upgraded until it became a popular stopping-off place for those travelling between Salisbury (now Harare) and Bulawayo, Rhodesia's second city. Dad, Stella and Gail (Barbi came a little later as I recall) lived next to the hotel in what can only be called a shack, with just an outside hole-in-the-ground loo. As was not uncommon at the time, we used torn-up strips of newspaper as toilet paper.

Of course, I lived with them only during the holidays, since I was sent to Guinea Fowl, a rural state boarding school near Gwelo (now Gweru) about fifty miles away.

Dad and I got on really well, especially considering that I had seen him so seldom during my first thirteen years. Stella did her best to treat me as a member of her family, though I know it was difficult for her at first, especially as I was resistant to her overtures and rather resentful of her presence. For months, since I was no longer able to call her Miss Fletcher, I called her nothing at all. At last Dad insisted that I call her Stella. Once I did so, the ice seemed to be broken and we got on much better after that.

Mom remained in Pretoria for about a year after I moved to Rhodesia. I think I went down to see her just once. There was no direct train link from Umvuma to South Africa. To travel by train would have meant being driven to Salisbury or Gwelo, then taking a train to Bulawayo, then the circuitous route though Bechuanaland (now Botswana) to Johannesburg. Then on another train from Jo'burg to Pretoria. Instead, Dad arranged for me to travel by road as a passenger in a very large and long truck with two trailers. In the back of the truck was some bedding which we slept in en route. When we got to Messina, the South African border town, we had to spend several days there, as the truck needed an axle part for which we had to wait. So it took most of a week to travel the six hundred miles from Umvuma to Pretoria.

Mom then moved on her own to Bulawayo, which meant that I now shared my holidays between Umvuma and Bulawayo.

She had found a job as a bookkeeper. Some months later, while she was sitting at her dressing table one evening, she said that she was expecting a visitor, Monty Lewin, who had asked her to marry him. Though I was rather shocked I did not express any opposition, as I wanted her to be happy.

Uncle Monty (as I was told to call him) was a bachelor in his forties and very set in his ways. He and I never really hit it off – I think we were both resentful of each other. Mom and Uncle Monty had a quiet civil wedding (I was not invited – I think I must have been at boarding school at the time) and then went to Pretoria to meet Mom's family. When they returned to Bulawayo, Uncle Monty was furious. He felt he and Mom had been insulted by the family, who had given them only some small kitchen gadget as a wedding present. He was a very unforgiving man and insisted that Mom break off all contact with her family. He threatened that unless I did the same I would no longer be allowed to see Mom. The reason I have no photos of my aunts, uncles and cousins and very few of myself as a young child is that Uncle Monty insisted that I destroy them all. It was as though the first fifteen years of my life were unimportant. Mom obeyed his commands, but I know she was deeply affected by having to sever all ties and contacts with her family.

Uncle Monty moved into Mom's one-bedroomed flat after their marriage. He had set up an import agency for tools and hardware imported mainly from the UK, Italy and Germany, and travelled throughout Rhodesia getting orders for his high-quality merchandise. Mom acted as his secretary and bookkeeper. He was undoubtedly a shrewd businessman and was very successful.

While they lived and worked in their small flat, I slept in the lounge on a short and narrow couch. Most evenings were spent playing canasta.

When I went to university, Uncle Monty was very opposed to the idea, but because I started doing a B.Com degree he was reconciled. But when towards the end of my first year I decided to become a teacher, he was furious and did his best to dissuade me. His method of persuasion (or in this case dissuasion) was to nag, threaten and bully. He thought I should become an accountant. Law (my original choice) and teaching were a waste of time, he felt, and would never make any money. At the end of my first year at Rhodes University he persuaded me to give accountancy a try and arranged for me to work during the main vacation (December to February) in an accountancy firm in Bulawayo. I found the work mind-numbingly boring. We spent nearly all day every day checking receipts and making sure that each company's books matched the piles of receipts. I could not see this as my life and returned to university at the start of the new academic year.

Because I had made up my mind to be a teacher, my fees were paid by the education department of the Southern Rhodesian government, though I now had the obligation to teach for a minimum of two years on completion of my course. This was just as well, since by that time Dad was struggling to pay the fees. To improve the hotel in Umvuma he had borrowed too much money and was having great difficulty in repaying his loan.

Uncle Monty's business meanwhile was flourishing. He and Mom decided to build a house in a new suburb of Bulawayo. It was a lovely single-storey house on an acre plot. It had three bedrooms and an office. Single-storey homes were the norm in Rhodesia and bear little resemblance to the typical bungalow in the UK.

On one occasion Mom parked her car, a fawn-coloured Peugeot 403, on a street in Bulawayo. After doing some shopping she returned to the car only to find that she could not get into it. She also noticed that a bag she had left on the back seat was missing. Convinced that someone had broken into the car, damaging the lock in the process, she summoned a policeman who also could not manage to open the door. He got out his notebook and started writing his report on the incident. As he called out the car's registration number, Mom realised that the car wasn't hers! Her own car was parked just a little further up the street.

Another storm was now brewing. Mom and Uncle Monty had married in a registry office and had not had a Jewish wedding. Since Uncle Monty was an atheist, this was hardly surprising. But with the birth of Vicki he felt it was important to get married according to the Jewish tradition, as otherwise, at least among orthodox Jews, she would be considered illegitimate. There was just one problem: my mother and father's divorce was also only a civil divorce, and a Jewish marriage was therefore not possible until the religious divorce too was carried out.

To obtain a Jewish divorce (or 'get') the husband has to go through a procedure in which certain declarations are made and documents prepared and signed before a rabbi. Anyway, at Uncle Monty's urging Mom asked Dad for a Jewish divorce. Dad naturally agreed, but in order to obtain it he had to travel to Salisbury to find a rabbi. Unfortunately, because of the financial problems he was having and the difficulty of leaving the hotel even for a day (at this stage he and Stella were running it on their own), he procrastinated. Weeks, maybe months, went by and he had not fulfilled his promise. Uncle Monty was justifiably furious and the delay simply fuelled his already low opinion of my father whom he regarded (wrongly in my view) as a good-for-nothing. I, of course, was the person on whom he unloaded all his bile. Eventually, he and Dad fixed on a day when Uncle Monty would drive down to Umvuma and personally take Dad to Salisbury to see the rabbi and obtain the divorce. This was duly done, but I was never allowed to forget my father's perfidy, a subject that came up almost every time Uncle Monty and I met.

Sometimes, Uncle Monty and Mom would leave me on my own in the house when they went on holiday. My job was to answer the phone and check the mail. I used to enjoy the freedom that Uncle Monty's absence gave. On one occasion (I guess it must have been before Vicki was born) Mom and Uncle Monty were returning from South Africa by car when they had an accident. Uncle Monty had suffered a heart attack while driving, causing the car to career off the road and crash into a wall. Fortunately neither of them was seriously hurt. Uncle Monty's doctor advised him to retire; so he began to run down his business.

Shortly thereafter, Vicki (Victoria Deborah), was born on New Year's Eve. Mom was in her forties and Uncle Monty must have been in his early fifties.

For a while Vicki's birth softened Uncle Monty, but it was not long before his bullying started again. One night, I was already in bed when I was woken by shouting. Uncle Monty was giving Mom a verbal battering, yelling at her about her family, about me, about my father. He threatened to throw her out of the house and said that he would make sure that she never saw Vicki again. I could hear Mom sobbing. I wanted to intervene, but my courage failed me. My brain also told me that my intervention might only have made matters worse. So I remained still until the crisis passed, but I never forgot this abuse of power. It helped to mould my attitude to bullying, an offence which I always dealt with promptly and firmly in my subsequent career.

Mom and I remained close, at least in spirit, but we were both always looking over our shoulder because of Uncle Monty's volatile nature.

I was very ashamed of my parents' divorce. Divorce was a much bigger issue in those days. As far as I knew, nobody else of my acquaintance had divorced parents. On one occasion Mom and I bumped into Ted Hanssen, one of my closest friends from school, who was visiting Bulawayo. I introduced Mom as Mrs Lewin without mentioning that she was my mother. Mom turned to Ted and said, "Mrs Lewin, Milton's mother." I nearly sank through the pavement, but was afterwards very ashamed of my behaviour. I felt like Peter denying Jesus!

The worst incidence of Uncle Monty's bullying was yet to come. It occurred many years later, towards the end of 1968, when I was living in Geneva and announced that I was marrying Marjorie Rebeiro, who was both an Indian and a Catholic. This infuriated Uncle Monty. He wrote me scathing letters demanding that I give up any such idea. Despite his avowed atheism, he could not accept my marrying a gentile, but his prejudice was not only religious (as stated) but also racial (as implied when he said that of course any Indian would regard it as a coup to marry a white man!). He threatened to prevent my seeing Mom and Vicki again if I went ahead with the marriage. Mom also appealed to me not to marry Marj, but I could see from her letter that she was acting under duress. Needless to say, our marriage went ahead and Uncle Monty carried out his threat.

As I subsequently found out, any letters that I wrote to Mom were intercepted and destroyed. She was forbidden to contact me. Even mention of my name was proscribed. After a year or so, I started receiving letters from Mom but was told to reply to a Poste Restante address in Cape Town. Without Uncle Monty's knowledge, Mom used to collect my letters from the post office. To do so she took a great risk, as Uncle Monty's reaction had he found out about the deception is too awful to contemplate.

After his death in (I think) 1974 or 1975, Mom immediately contacted us. She called the school in Geneva who informed her that we had moved to the UK, but fortunately they gave her a contact address and phone number. As soon as possible thereafter she visited us in Stroud where our nursery school was located. This was the first time she had met her grandchildren and Marj.

Thereafter Mom visited us every couple of years. However, I would not return to South Africa until apartheid was ended. Apart from my repugnance towards this evil system, I felt that it would be wrong to visit that country until my wife could do so too as an equal citizen. Thus my first visit to South Africa (though without Marj) was not until 1995, when I returned to celebrate Mom's eightieth birthday.

Subsequently, Marj and I visited South Africa every few years (on three occasions for the weddings of my nephews Evan,

Justin and Claude, and of my niece Hayley). In 2004, we were accompanied by André, Nathalie and Emilie. Thus Mom was able to meet her first great-grandchild.

As usual, that year we had arranged a house swap. We stayed in a large house with a swimming pool in Bergvliet, a comfortable Cape Town suburb. The visit was particularly memorable as we hosted a party for both sides of my family. Thus my three sisters, together with their spouses and children, all came. Most importantly, both Mom and Stella were there, the first time they had seen each other since before my parents' divorce. What is more, they got on very well together. It was a wonderful act of reconciliation, which did great credit to both of them.

A year later, Stella died. Then, early in 2007, Mom died at the age of ninety-one. In her last couple of years she had become very frail, though her mind was still clear and active to the end. She had been taken to hospital a few days before and seemed to be on the mend, but she then died of a sudden heart attack while she was sitting up in bed.

Having just visited Mom in November, I did not travel to South Africa for her funeral, a decision I later regretted. But at the time I felt that I had at least had the opportunity to say goodbye to her. Later, for the 'unveiling' (hakamat ha-matzeivah in Hebrew) of the memorial stone, Marj and I did attend. As the oldest (indeed only) son, I had a part to play in the service. But just as the rabbi started speaking, much to my extreme embarrassment, my mobile phone rang. Since everyone I knew in South Africa was gathered around the graveside I had not thought it was necessary to switch it off. It was in fact my sister Barbi (Dad's daughter) who was looking for the grave in this vast cemetery. I will not forget this moment. If the grave had been open I think I would have jumped in.

Mom had a long and often difficult life. She came from a poor but strong family. Her first marriage failed and she brought me up alone. The man she subsequently fell in love with turned out to be an alcoholic. Her attempted suicide led to her losing her job and her son. Her second marriage, after she moved to Rhodesia, was not an easy one. For the sake of her daughter she loyally supported her husband until his death. I think the happiest years of her life were those spent as a widow. She and Vicki had a wonderful relationship, and Mom was adored by Vicki's children. Vicki and her husband Jonathan gave her unstinting support and I know Mom felt loved and wanted.

Even though circumstances kept us apart for many years, Mom and I retained a close bond. Her death was a great loss, but I feel fortunate to have had such a warm and loving mother.

Sisters

My three younger sisters (more accurately, half-sisters) whom I love dearly all live in or near Cape Town. Gail and Barbi (Barbara) are the children of Dad and Stella, and Vicki (Victoria) is the child of Mom and Uncle Monty. Circumstances, distance, a wide age gap, and in Vicki's case, her father's prohibition against having any contact with me, meant that we did not spend a great deal of time together. Yet that does not seem to matter in the way we feel about each other. Our affection, which I know is mutual, seems unaffected by such obstacles.

Gail, the eldest, naturally spent more time with me while growing up. Her husband Bob Gotte sadly died very young. Gail was left with a young son Evan, who is just a little younger than André. Gail had a successful career with a computer company. She now lives with her partner Paul (who is a few years younger than Gail) in Kleinmond, a small seaside town not far from Cape Town. Evan is married to Chayne (who would have been classified as 'coloured' under the despicable apartheid regime) and has two daughters, Imogen and Chloe.

Since Dad's wife Stella was a gentile, both Gail and Barbi were brought up as nominally Christian. Barbi, however, met and fell in love with Davide Hanan, a Sephardic Jew whose French-speaking family originated from Turkey. This meant that Barbi had to undergo the intensive process of converting to Judaism. Like many converts she is now an enthusiastic Jewish woman. She and Davide have two sons, Mikael and Claude. Davide's computer business thrived and was bought out by a multinational firm at the height of the computer boom. This, together with Davide's continuing entrepreneurial skills, has left them very well off. They live in a clifftop house on the slopes of Table Mountain overlooking Bantry Bay. Barbi has a consuming interest in art. We have two of her early watercolours in our home.

At Cape Town University, Vicki obtained a degree in accountancy. There she also met her future husband, Jonathan Palte, a fellow accountancy student. Vicki and Jonathan have three children: Justin, who runs his own IT firm and is married to Samantha; Hayley, who married her long-term boyfriend, Mesut (a Turkish Muslim) in a Jewish marriage ceremony; and Lauren, an artist, who married her Christian boyfriend, Chad.

So our family has certainly played its part in multiculturalism, integrating faiths, races and nationalities!

Friends

Probably the best thing about boarding school is that one makes friends for life. Although most of my friends from that era have now died, I still remember them with great affection. Once I left Rhodesia I lost contact with most of them. Unlike Marj I am not good at keeping in touch. Despite this, our friendships endured. Whenever we subsequently met we just seemed to pick up where we had left off.

My greatest friend throughout school and university, and the person I most admired, was Barry van Blomestein. Barry started with the advantage of being extremely good-looking but without any vanity. He was a natural athlete and was particularly good at cricket, ending up as captain of the First XI. He was also selected as a member of the Rhodesian Nuffield cricket team. This was a team that was chosen annually from all the schools throughout Rhodesia and toured South Africa during the summer holidays. He later also played hockey at the provincial level.

Barry became Head Boy at Guinea Fowl. He never asserted his authority, but nobody ever resisted him. He treated everyone alike and had a great sense of fairness. He never sought popularity but it just seemed to accompany him everywhere. He had just one steady girlfriend at school (Monica Booysens); then at university he again went out with just one girl (the lovely Shirley Orr). At Rhodes he majored in mathematics and geography. On graduation he became a teacher in Umtali (now Mutare), a beautiful town in the eastern highlands of Rhodesia. There he married and had several children, later moving to Natal.

Ours was an unequal friendship. Although I am sure that Barry would have acknowledged me as one of his best friends, I simply worshipped him and placed him on a pedestal, from which – as far as I know – he never fell. Barry died far too young of cancer.

Gordon Phillips was just over four feet tall. Inevitably at Guinea Fowl School he was called Shorty, not in a mean way, but it nevertheless must have hurt to be reminded of his stature every time someone spoke to him.

He had a splendid voice, a booming bass, as he grew older. His most memorable singing role was as Gaspard in *Les Cloches de Corneville*.

Passionate about cricket, he bowled a tricky leg-break. When I left Guinea Fowl he took my place as scorer for the First XI. His passion for cricket led to his becoming a member of the MCC at Lords in later life. He also wrote articles about cricket and co-authored *The Wisden Book of Cricket Memorabilia*.

Gordon and I were also together at Rhodes University where he studied law. On moving to the UK, Gordon became the archivist of *The Times* for twelve years. He later began writing books and was in constant demand by companies and guilds to write their histories.

Gordon married twice, but both marriages failed. I liked both his wives, but Gordon suffered from depression (in the days when the treatment was 'pull your socks up') and must have been a difficult person to live with.

Gordon was great at keeping in touch with people, organising a couple of memorable reunions of our university friends and school friends.

He died in 2003 at the age of 66. His funeral in his beloved Wales, where he lived for his last two years, was attended by friends from all parts of his life: school, university, *The Times*, the MCC and many others. *The Times* published an obituary.

Churchill School, where I taught for eight happy years, had a great collegiate spirit among the staff, particularly among its younger members. Two friends really stand out for me: Paul Hjul and Willie Marais, who taught history and Afrikaans respectively. Like me, they were tremendously conscientious and devoted almost every waking hour to the school. Paul became the housemaster of the boarding house. In addition he ran the pipe band. This was the headmaster's pride and joy, and Paul ensured that the band reached new heights, taking it several times to Scotland and the Edinburgh Tattoo. After I left Churchill and went abroad, I heard that Paul had tragically died while in Johannesburg. I was told that he had fallen to his death, which was possibly suicide. The news of his death came as a great shock to me, but at the time I made no attempt to find out more.

As I have mentioned elsewhere, Willie Marais and I worked closely together on the production of several musicals at Churchill. He directed the productions while I was the musical director. In many ways our roles should have been reversed, for Willie became an enthusiastic pianist. He spent his sabbatical leave in London at the Royal Academy of Music in the hope that he would improve enough to become a professional musician, but decided in the end that he had left it too late. For a few years we also shared a house together with another colleague, Martin Sinclair. Willie was a farmer at heart; so it was no surprise that he bought a smallholding of some fifteen acres. He married Annette, a delightful young woman, and they lived in a very basic house on their farm while Willie continued teaching at Churchill. After I moved to Switzerland I heard that Willie had died of a heart attack.

The position of headmaster of a school makes it difficult to form friendships with colleagues, for you are always their boss, but I can say that since my retirement several of my former colleagues have remained good friends. Jane Treftz, the first principal of Southbank's Hampstead branch, has continued to keep in regular touch. She has always been most supportive and helpful. Mary Langford, who ran the admissions department at Southbank, has also remained in touch and is someone I believe I can count among my friends. Another is Brett Goldspink, a much younger teacher (he is the same age as my son André). He has turned out to be a staunch friend. We first met when Brett was a young teacher at Southbank and had nowhere to live; so Marj and I offered to accommodate him for a while. We seemed to have a lot in common and have remained firm friends since my retirement. I was honoured to be invited to speak at the celebration of his civil partnership with Herman.

Bella

While Marj was teaching at a local private nursery school, the headmistress's dog gave birth to a litter of puppies. We were given the opportunity of having one and chose Bella, a silky black, mainly, cocker spaniel. She had a delightful temperament, gentle and friendly. The children loved her, though they soon grew tired of taking her for walks.

As a puppy she destroyed our dining room carpet by chewing all the edges, as well as gnawing at the legs of the furniture. Marj faithfully took her for walks including a daily outing to Wimbledon Common. I would help at weekends. She (I'm referring to Bella) loved water and would jump into the ponds at every opportunity, especially to retrieve a ball.

Although generally obedient she loved to swim after ducks, emitting a sound that was more like a quack than a bark. On one occasion she chased deer in Bushey Park for more than an hour while we vainly and desperately tried to call her back. At last she just bounded back to us. We were lucky not to have been fined for failing to keep her under control.

On another occasion, during a walk on Wimbledon Common, Bella just disappeared. We spent hours looking for her. Night drew in and we still had not found her. We contacted the park warden who kindly helped us in our search. At about 10.00 p.m we gave up and returned home. The only shred of hope was the reassurance given by the warden who said that they had never yet lost a dog on the common.

After a restless night we got up early to resume our search. We were just having breakfast when Nathalie came through to say that she had found Bella on the front doorstep. Bella was totally exhausted, dripping with sweat, her coat all matted and filthy. Somehow she had found her way back from the common to our house (about three miles by car, a route she had never walked). She, however, must have walked many more miles, as I understand that dogs find their way by walking in circles until they pick up a scent. Needless to say, after a little food, Bella just slept the rest of the day.

When we moved from our house in Wimbledon to a flat in Maida Vale, Bella was already quite old. Her barking might have disturbed other residents in the block, but because she was becoming increasingly deaf, she no longer heard the postman or the doorbell; so she very seldom barked. She died peacefully in June 2001 at the age of eighteen.

My Passions

Apart from my family, the things that have motivated me most as an adult have been education, music, theatre and cooking.

I was able to indulge my passion for education throughout my working life through teaching and running schools. Founding Southbank International School was of course the highlight of my career and gave me the opportunity of putting into effect, with the help of all my colleagues, ideas accumulated over the years.

My first taste of 'classical' music did not occur until I was a teenager at Guinea Fowl School. Even then it was only the music of Arthur Sullivan (after seeing a performance of The *Mikado* at Chaplin School) and Planquette who wrote the music for *Les Cloches de Corneville*, an operetta that we put on at Guinea Fowl. I also enjoyed some of the pieces that I was learning to play on the piano: a Brahms Hungarian dance and Schubert's *Marche Militaire*.

It was not until I was at university that I really had the chance to hear classical music. Nineteen fifty-six was my last year at Rhodes and was also the bicentenary of Mozart's birth. Two performances in Grahamstown stand out: Mozart's Requiem and his Piano Concerto in D Minor (K466). My memory, which may just be wishful thinking, says that the latter was played by Clara Haskil. Whether true or not, hearing this sublime music was an extraordinarily uplifting experience.

During my second year at Rhodes, I had one of the best holidays of my life. Four of us hitchhiked up to the Hogsback

Mountains, where the parents of one of the students had a primitive shack with no electricity. We had to chop firewood and cook our own food. The scenery was breathtaking, but the best part of the holiday for me was the discovery of a huge collection of 78 rpm records of Verdi operas, which we played on a wind-up gramophone. There, for the first time, I heard *Rigoletto* and *Il Trovatore*. I was mesmerized by the voices of Gallicurci and Gigli, and overwhelmed by the glorious quartet 'Bella figlia dell'amore'. I was now totally hooked on opera.

It has always saddened me that Marj does not share my love of opera. Perhaps if I had introduced her gradually to the genre she might have felt differently, but I made the mistake, when we were just married, of taking her to a performance of Wagner's *Parsifal* at the Grand Théâtre in Geneva. (I have to confess that even I found the production tedious.) It was only later that I read the quote, "*Parsifal* – the kind of opera that starts at six o'clock and after it has been going three hours, you look at your watch and it says 6:20."

I had learnt to play the piano as a child, but I never enjoyed it. My first teacher was one who liked to rap your knuckles with a ruler whenever you played a wrong note. Then I attended lessons at a music studio near Mom's work in Pretoria. The method used was one called 'Syncopation'. You read only the treble clef and with your left hand played only chords. I never got the hang of it, and the result was that I did not learn the bass clef. Once I joined Guinea Fowl School, I had a good teacher, Mrs Williams, but I practised very little. My main reason for taking piano lessons there was to enable me to miss the dreaded PT (Physical Training) lessons. Mrs Williams was complicit in this scheme, and I don't believe the PT teacher minded my absence from his classes.

A few years after retiring I decided to take up the piano again. Of course, I wish I had been more diligent as a child, but now I practise regularly and am making reasonable progress. John Prentice is a first-rate teacher. The highlight of my musical year is the annual summer school for pianists held at Chetham's School of Music in Manchester in August. This summer school is for pianists of all abilities and describes itself as the friendliest summer school in the world, and I believe it is. In addition to individual lessons there are masterclasses, seminars and several concerts a day. You are encouraged to attend the lessons given to other students. Both students and staff (many of whom are internationally renowned pianists) eat together in the dining room. The talk is constantly of music and you are surrounded by the sound of music emanating from every corner of the school.

I also love the theatre. At school and university I acted in several plays, while as a teacher in both Rhodesia and later, at the Institut auf dem Rosenberg in Switzerland, I directed a number of plays. At Southbank I encouraged both drama and music. And I love to attend live theatre whenever I have the chance.

I have always enjoyed cooking. My mother was an excellent cook of simple, traditional food in the Jewish East European tradition. So latkes, chopped liver, gefilte fish, kneidlach and tzimmes were dishes that were part of my childhood and that I still love.

When staying with Dad in Umvuma, I used to spend a lot of time in the hotel kitchen. There I think I developed my love of cooking. The African chef, known unimaginatively as Cookie, sometimes let me help prepare simple dishes, but I got into trouble on one occasion when I emptied a whole bottle of orange squash into the Scotch broth. Soup had to be removed from that day's menu. At Rhodes I used to cook curry and rice on a small gas ring, which for some unknown reason was on the floor of one of the bathrooms. My friends seemed to enjoy the dish.

I am an adventurous cook, and love trying out new dishes or varying old favourites. Sometimes the results are dire, but I have always been a risk-taker. You learn more from your mistakes than from your successes.

Conference notes

While attending the International Baccalaureate conference in Ottawa, I decided to catch a bus. You enter the bus from the front and a notice there tells you to place $1.40 (exact fare only) into the receptacle. Not having the exact fare, I politely asked the driver if it would be OK if I placed $2.00 in the receptacle instead. With great hostility he replied, "I don't speak French." I guess my English/South African accent must have seemed unintelligible to him, but I think it is an illustration of the ill feeling at that time towards French-speaking Canadians in that part of the country, right on the border of Ontario and Quebec.

Then there was the occasion when Jane Treftz, Gwen Martinez and I attended a European Council of International Schools (ECIS) conference in The Hague. When we landed at Schiphol Airport we piled all our luggage onto a trolley and made our way to the exit. I was convinced that Schiphol's escalators were designed to accommodate luggage trolleys. I must have confused it with another airport (Zurich, I think), but I was as determined as a TomTom satnav in insisting that I was right. So imagine the scene as we descended the escalator, the three of us desperately trying to prevent this overloaded trolley from tumbling down the escalator. Even at the time it seemed hilarious, although it could have been disastrous. But the image that remains with me is the pained expression of blind panic on Jane's face. That, I think, is when she decided not to rely on my judgment and to make her own decisions.

I was twice nominated as a member of the board of ECIS, but was twice rejected. I think it was because I spoke out strongly against two proposals made by the then Executive Secretary of ECIS. The first was his proposal to move the ECIS headquarters from the UK to Nice in France. I was not opposed in principle, but it meant that several loyal and valuable members of staff would have to lose their jobs, and there seemed to be no compelling reason for the move, just an understandable preference for the glamour of the Mediterranean over the more subtle charms of Hampshire. I am pleased to say that ECIS remained in Petersfield, at least for the next ten years. My second objection was to the proposal that ECIS should be split, one part becoming an international organisation, the other a European one. I felt this would be an unnecessary waste of resources. I lost this battle, but I still believe that those of us who argued for the maintenance of ECIS as a single body were right.

Religious Beliefs

Although I was born into a Jewish family, I had essentially a secular upbringing. On both sides of my family Jewish rituals were largely ignored. We did not observe Jewish dietary laws, nor did we go to the synagogue except for weddings and other special occasions. My bar mitzvah was the most intensive association I had with Judaism as a religion, but even that was more concerned with learning the Hebrew texts required for the event than studying the religion itself. Yet the stories of the Bible did form an important part of my education, and I am grateful for that. While we celebrated Pesach (the Passover) and Rosh Hashanah (the Jewish New Year) and now and then fasted on Yom Kippur (the Day of Atonement), we also celebrated Christmas with a lot of enthusiasm.

At Christian Brothers College, all the Jewish boys were exempted from religious studies, though we could not help picking up snippets of Catholic doctrine. At Guinea Fowl School, as the only Jewish pupil in the school, I was not required to attend the daily assembly or the Religious Knowledge classes, but I chose to do so, and I am glad I did. It helped me understand that we may all have different beliefs, some of which I might reject, but that we can nonetheless respect each other. This realisation has played a fundamental part in my life and has been the basis of my educational philosophy. And I loved the hymns that we sang every morning at assembly.

One of the clubs I attended at Guinea Fowl was the Christian Union, and for a while I was tempted to become a Christian, but eventually I rejected the idea. I was who I was, and conversion would not have changed this.

Throughout my childhood I never questioned the existence of God. Even though the question 'Who made God?' remained unanswered (and still remains unanswered), I have never really doubted His existence.

As an adult I have lived a very secular life. Formal religion has played no part in my life, nor have I attempted to influence my children's religious beliefs. Having married a Catholic, I have never tried to influence Marj's beliefs. Yet, with only occasional doubts, I still believe in God, at least in the gentle, kind and just God of my imagination.

Politics

I have always been fascinated by politics, though I have never joined a political party. My views have generally been at the liberal end of the political spectrum. When growing up in South Africa and Rhodesia, I always questioned the race laws long before it was fashionable to do so. It always seemed wrong to me that race (or indeed religion) should play any part in determining who could do what.

At my all-white boarding school, both in the debating society and in the dormitory, I argued strongly for equality. Of course, with so little contact with non-whites, it was difficult to envisage what society would be like if all discrimination were outlawed, but nevertheless the theory seemed right to me. I used to quote the doctrine expressed by Cecil John Rhodes: "Equal rights to all civilised men". At that time I did not perceive the sting in the tail of that tenet: who was 'civilised' and did the word 'men' include women?

While apartheid in South Africa was completely abhorrent to me, events in Rhodesia seemed to be moving, albeit slowly, in the right direction. The University College of Rhodesia and Nyasaland had opened as a multiracial university under the auspices of the University of London. Garfield Todd, a former missionary from New Zealand, had become Prime Minister of Southern Rhodesia in 1953. He was pushing to widen the franchise by lowering the property qualifications that had previously prevented most blacks from acquiring the right to vote. African education was being extended. Some prestigious all-white private schools began to admit a few black pupils.

To me these were heady days, and I was an enthusiastic supporter of Garfield Todd. Unfortunately, he was moving too fast for the majority of the mainly white electorate, and Garfield Todd was deposed by his own party. The subsequent break-up of the Federation of Rhodesia and Nyasaland left Southern Rhodesia isolated. The emergence of a rather reactionary government under Ian Smith led to UDI, the Unilateral Declaration of Independence, on Armistice Day 1965. The collapse of all my hopes and dreams of a liberal Rhodesia was the direct cause of my decision to leave the country. Later, a rebellion among many blacks and a destructive guerilla war that lasted for fifteen years until the establishment of Zimbabwe in 1980 resulted in untold horrors in that beautiful country. The election under universal suffrage of Robert Mugabe as Prime Minister (later President) initially showed some promise, but his regime soon turned into one of the most cruel and corrupt in Africa. Despite occasional signs of emerging from this dark chapter in its turbulent history, Zimbabwe remains a country in crisis.

Influences

In growing up, the greatest influence on me was undoubtedly my mother. She gave me my values through her unconditional love. Every decision she made was reached in what she believed was my interests. I was never chastised, except on one occasion when Mom slapped my face. I think it was for a disparaging remark I made about our lodger (who, unbeknown to me, was Mom's lover). I remember the slap only because it came as such a shock and seemed so out of character, but I am sure I must have deserved it, for Mom's patience was remarkable.

Sadly, Mom's influence waned when, after her suicide attempt when I was thirteen, I was sent to live with my father in Rhodesia. Or, rather, I was sent to boarding school and shared my school holidays between Mom and Dad. Once Mom remarried, her influence over me largely ended, as I did not get on with Uncle Monty, her new husband.

Dad's influence was almost negligible during my first thirteen years. I saw very little of him. I always loved him and was always hoping to see more of him. Even after I discovered around the age of ten or eleven that my parents were divorced, I would pray every night that they would get together again.

Once Dad became my guardian (I don't think this was an official status) at the age of thirteen, I had more contact with him. But I would say he seldom tried to influence me, relying instead on the school to shape my life. Dad was a benign presence in my life, but I cannot recall any attempt at guidance or advice.

At Guinea Fowl School I suppose that my friends were my greatest influence. First my heroes – Michael Darroch and then Barry van Blomestein. (My admiration for Barry remained undimmed through school, university and beyond.) Then some of my friends – in particular Alan Ruffell – with whom I had a close and easy bond throughout my time at Guinea Fowl.

Among my teachers, the most influential was our brilliant mathematics teacher, Bob Klette. He not only sparked my interest in mathematics but also helped me believe that I should always raise my sights and aim higher.

At Rhodes University there was only one lecturer that really inspired me. That was Professor F G Butler, the professor of English at the university. I still remember his inspiring inaugural address called 'An Aspect of Tragedy'. He certainly sparked my interest in English literature.

Once I started teaching I suppose the greatest influence was the headmaster of the first school at which I taught. E J 'Jeeves' Hougaard was the founding head of Churchill School. Although I rejected his strict disciplinary approach (including corporal punishment), his total commitment to the welfare of his students, his high expectations, his ability to inspire and to build school spirit – these were all attributes that I greatly admired.

In my own teaching career, several great educators have influenced my methods: I was very excited by WHD Rouse's book on teaching Latin by the direct method and by the teaching methods used by the Perse School in Cambridge. Both these methods greatly influenced my teaching.

I also read *The Play Way* by Henry Caldwell Cook, who taught English at the Perse School. I was so stimulated by his approach to teaching English that I resolved to use his methods if I were ever given the chance. And indeed I did so when I taught briefly at Lord Malvern School.

The greatest influence on my philosophy of education was undoubtedly John Holt, particularly his first two books, *How*

Children Fail and *How Children Learn*, as well as *The Underachieving School*. His understanding of children was extraordinary. We need to trust children to find their own way of learning, to respect their views and provide them with direct experiences. The force-feeding of children may work for a while, but it does not create people for whom learning is a lifelong joy.

This too was the philosophy of the great Japanese educator Shinichi Suzuki. The very title of his book *Nurtured by Love* describes the essence of his philosophy. That is the reason that Suzuki violin lessons were introduced at Southbank for every child in the primary school. The method is entirely experiential – the children learn to play the instrument by playing it, long before they learn to read music. In a way this is so obvious: we learn to drive by driving, not by reading a manual; and we learn to cook by cooking, not by reading a cookbook. Of course we benefit from guidance and encouragement, but it's the doing that is most important.

Another important influence was A S Neill, the founder of Summerhill School. Neill's belief that children should be happy is so obvious, yet so often ignored. To achieve happiness in children he thought that the right path was through the freedom to make their own decisions. Neill may have carried these principles to extremes, but nevertheless they provide an ideal which educators need to bear in mind.

And of course the book that provided the inspiration for starting Southbank was *A School without Walls* by John Bremer and Michael von Moschzisker. This gave us the idea of using London as the classroom, based on Philadelphia's Parkway Program. Despite the inevitable limitations of time, money and other expectations, it always remained important at Southbank for teachers to look outwards and use the many opportunities provided by a great city like London to further their pupils' education.

Desert Island Discs

One of my favourite radio programmes is *Desert Island Discs* on BBC Radio Four. Each week an individual (usually a celebrity or someone distinguished) is interviewed and asked to select eight records that they would like if they were alone on a desert island. They are also asked to choose one luxury and a book (they are given the Bible and the complete works of Shakespeare).

Since I will never be asked onto the programme, here are my choices (I've given myself the licence to choose ten records):

1. Mozart: 2nd movement of the Piano Concerto in D minor (K466), preferably played by Clara Haskill. This was the first piece of classical music that I really heard when I was at Rhodes University. After hearing this I was hooked and I love it still.

2. Verdi: the quartet 'Bella figlia dell'amore' from Rigoletto. In a strange way this reminds me of my children, because I used to try to sing this in the bath and they would immediately call out, "Oh no!" and close their ears.

3. Schubert: 'An die Musik'. When I lived in Rhodesia there was a weekly radio programme of classical music – I think it was the only broadcast of classical music on Rhodesia Radio. It was always introduced by 'An die Musik' played on the piano on a recording specially made for the programme by the famous accompanist Gerald Moore. I love this piece of music and indeed all Schubert's songs.

4. Richard Strauss: 'Beim Schlafengehen' from his Four Last Songs. I first heard this in a wonderful television programme in which Dame Kiri te Kanawa rehearses the songs with Sir Georg Solti. The music sent shivers down my spine and it still does. It is one of the pieces I have chosen for my funeral.

5. Dvorak: first movement of his Cello Concerto in B minor. At one point the music swells gloriously. It definitely has the tingle factor.

6. Al Jolson: 'Sonny Boy'. Ever since I saw the film *The Jolson Story* as a boy, I have been a fan of his. I know that the way he used to blacken his face is now considered disrespectful and even racist, but that was not true at the time. I would say just shut your eyes and listen to him sing. This song is a tribute to my son André and, in its sad ending, a reminder of my daughter Nathalie.

7. Verdi again. This time the glorious 'Willow Song' from his *Otello*, sung by Desdemona just before she is murdered by her husband. And if it is possible to sneak in a little of the 'Ave Maria' that immediately follows, so much the better.

8. Gilbert and Sullivan: 'A Magnet Hung in a Hardware Shop' from *Patience*. When I was a young teacher at Churchill School in Salisbury, Rhodesia, my friend Willie Marais and I put on *Patience* with our students (all boys). Despite being almost musically illiterate, I conducted the orchestra of mainly semi-professional musicians thanks to a week-long crash course given by Eileen Reynolds, Principal of the Rhodesian College of Music. I enjoy all of Gilbert and Sullivan, but *Patience* holds a special place in my heart.

9. Mozart: 'La ci darem la mano' from *Don Giovanni*. My list would have been incomplete without some music from a Mozart

opera. His genius, consummate in every genre of music, is just incomparable.

10. Puccini: 'Vissi d'arte' from *Tosca*. The first film of an opera that I ever saw was *Tosca*, with Franco Corelli as Cavaradossi, and I was just blown away by the music. 'Vissi d'arte', which Tosca sings just before she kills the wicked Scarpia in defence of her honour, is always so moving. Maria Callas would be my preferred Tosca.

Guests on Desert Island Discs are always asked which disc they would save if they were allowed only one. Mine would have to be 'Bella figlia dell'amore', because of its associations and four wonderful voices.

Although it may seem a bit pretentious, my book would be Vergil's *Aeneid*. Not only is it a stirring and magnificent poem, but Aeneas's experience as a wanderer might give me some tips on survival. As my Latin is now rather rusty, I would need an edition of the *Aeneid* with a good translation alongside. (Robert Fitzgerald's translation is one I have always enjoyed.)

As for my luxury, I am torn between a piano and a regular supply of fresh bed linen. In the end I think I have to opt for the piano.

Retracing my Roots

The weddings of my nieces and nephews in Cape Town have given us the excuse to visit South Africa several times. We generally do a house swap, which enables us to live comfortably like a local without breaking the bank.

On one occasion, Marj and I started our journey in East London, which is on the east coast of South Africa between Port Elizabeth and Durban. Just outside East London is Gonubie Mouth, where Dad ran his first hotel. Dad was buried in East London, and I wanted to visit his grave. It was not easy to find, but eventually we discovered it in the Jewish cemetery attached to the main cemetery. It was a sad sight. The part of the cemetery where he is buried was bare and neglected. We placed a stone, brought from the beach at Eastbourne, on his gravestone. (We had brought two stones, the second to be placed on Mom's grave in Cape Town.)

We had hired a car, and on the long drive from East London to Cape Town stopped off at Grahamstown, where I was able to visit my alma mater. Rhodes University has grown enormously since I was a student there, but architecturally it has retained its charm and is a beautiful, though much extended, campus.

Then in December 2013, visiting Cape Town for the fourth wedding in the series (two more to go!) we took the famous Blue Train from Cape Town to Pretoria, a thousand miles to the north. There, after much searching, I had arranged to meet several of my cousins whom I had not seen since my early teens.

Meeting my cousins was very emotional. Neville came the

first afternoon. He drove us around a bit. Then Ivan and his wife Marie spent Friday morning with us. They got on so well with Marj. When I told them of my plan to have a taxi drive us to all the addresses I knew from my childhood, they insisted on taking us themselves. They were excellent guides and were certainly better than any taxi service would have been.

Then on Saturday morning Jeffrey (with his ex-wife Karen) and Rhona came to see us. Jeffrey, Rhona and I had lived together in the same house with Mom and Auntie Faye during the war when our fathers were in the army. Maureen, Auntie Seema's daughter, was unable to come as she had no transport, but we had a long chat on the phone.

I hope that in the future we will all keep in touch with each other. They were an important part of my first thirteen years.

Postscript

As my life enters its closing chapter, I find myself considering whether it was all worthwhile.

Do I have regrets? Yes, of course I do. I regret my parents' divorce, but without it I would not have my three lovely sisters (half-sisters, if I'm to be pedantic).

I regret my mother's suicide attempt, which led to my being separated from my family and sent to boarding school. Yet at Guinea Fowl School and subsequently Rhodes University I made great lifelong friends even though nearly all of them are now dead.

I regret the political developments in what was then Rhodesia, which led to the election of a racist government and the Unilateral Declaration of Independence. This made me decide to leave Rhodesia. But how can I regret this? Had I not done so, I would not have met the most important person in my life, my wife Marj, nor would I have had my two wonderful children, Nathalie and André, nor my three beautiful grandchildren, Emilie, Emma and Léo.

Nor would I have had the opportunity of founding Southbank International School, which is my greatest professional achievement.

So no, I can have no serious regrets, except one: the untimely death of my beloved daughter, Nathalie. For this there is no upside and no solace. Time may make grief more bearable, but it is always there.

I glance again at the old man. Yes, there is joy in his face and a twinkle in his eye. But behind the sparkle I can catch just a glimpse of the pain.